AN INTRODUCTION TO
TAXATION IN KENYA

An introduction to
TAXATION IN KENYA

by

SAFDAR ALI BUTT
B Com, M Com, FICA, FSCT, FAAI, CI
Lecturer, Kenya Institute of Administration
Lower Kabete, Kenya

and

AMIRALI SOKWALA
ACCA
Lecturer, Mombasa Polytechnic
Mombasa, Kenya

CASSELL . LONDON

CASSELL & COMPANY LIMITED
35 Red Lion Square, London WC1R 4SG
and at Sydney, Auckland, Toronto, Johannesburg

An affiliate of Macmillan Inc., New York

First published 1978

I.S.B.N. 0 304 29999 5

Printed and bound in Great Britain at
The Camelot Press Ltd, Southampton

PREFACE

It is with a tinge of sense of pride that we present this book which we believe is the first on the subject in Kenya. A number of Kenyan (and at least one overseas) examination bodies, both in the field of Accountancy and Secretaryship, require their students to write a paper on Kenya Taxation or otherwise have a knowledge of its principles and practice. So far, the students and all others who wished to study this subject had only the Income Tax Act (Cap. 470) to resort to. While this Act is undisputedly the source of almost all information concerning income tax matters, it is, we believe, often beyond the powers of an average person to get the message lying behind a battery of legal and sophisticated terms. Some who have that power may, on occassions, be too busy to devote a substantial slice of their precious time to scanning every section of the Act in search of a piece of information. It is to assist all these persons that we have made a humble attempt at presenting the subject in a simplified and easily understandable language.

A good number of worked examples have been given to assist not only the students in solving the examination problems but also the businessmen and practising accountants to get an insight into the practical aspects of the subject.

At the time this book went to press, no amendments had been made in the Income Tax Act to accommodate any changes that may arise from the dissolution of the East African Community. The book is therefore based on the 1977 revision of the Act with an exception of Schedule Three that lists tax rates. Most of the problems given in the book are based on the rates that become effective on 1st January 1978.

We have made every attempt to secure factual accuracy, but we will be grateful if teachers and students of this subjects, or others concerned with it will kindly notify us of any area where they will wish an improvement to be made when the next edition is printed.

Our sincere thanks are due to Mr J.G. Johnston, Secretary, the Kenya Accountants and Secretaries National Examinations Board, and Mr J.V. Wanjala, Senior Lecturer, the Kenya Institute of Administration, Lower Kabete, for their very useful suggestions. Grateful acknowledgement is also made to the KASNEB for kindly permitting us to include their past examination papers as an appendix to this book.

12 August 1977

P.O. Box 47811,
Nairobi, Kenya.

S.A. *Butt*
A. *Sokwala*

CONTENTS

Chapter One

INTRODUCTION

WHY TAXES?

The government of Kenya like any other government provides a number of free or subsidized services to its people, e.g. education, health, maintenance of law and order, defence, assistance to farmers and businessmen, etc. These services require a lot of finance. A very small part of this finance is derived from the few profit-making ventures run by the government, e.g. state-owned commercial banks, but for a large portion of it, it is necessary to levy taxes. One very simple justification for levying taxes is that since a government is run for the benefit of its people, its expenditure must be borne by the people.

PRINCIPLES OF TAXATION

A government is guided by several principles in determining what taxes should be levied, by whom should they be payable and what rates should be imposed. Some of these principles are:

1. Taxes should not have any adverse effect on the supply of economic resources—labour, capital, etc. For example a very high rate of income tax may prove a disincentive to work beyond a certain level as an employee may feel that additional labour will not fetch him sufficient financial reward. Again if a government levies heavy export tax on any commodity it may simply become too expensive for a potential importer resulting in reduced exports and hence reduced foreign exchange earnings.

2. Taxes should be easy to collect and not easy to evade. High cost of tax collection, or possibility of large scale tax evasion, may defeat the very purpose for which they are levied—namely to raise revenue.

3. Taxes should not cause any hardship to the taxpayer. For example an import duty of, say, 500% imposed on an essential commodity like medicine will easily put it out of the reach of a common man, causing him undue suffering.
4. It is often deemed desirable to use income tax, and certain other taxes, as a tool to ensure an equitable distribution of wealth in the country. By imposing heavy tax rate on larger incomes and luxury items, and by imposing no or very little tax on things needed by the poorer section of the population, a government aims to alleviate the problems of later group. It is no secret that most of the free services provided by the government like medical treatment at government hospitals, primary education upto Standard IV, etc. are utilized by the poor. Money to provide these services comes mainly from the better-off section of the country's population.

TYPES OF TAXES

Taxes may be classified in two ways: according to impact and incidence and according to the base. Classified according to impact and incidence, taxes may be *Direct* or *Indirect*. Classified according to base, taxes may be on *income*, on *capital* or on *expenditure*. Each type is briefly discussed below.

Direct Taxes

A tax is said to be direct when its impact and incidence are on the same person. The impact of a tax is on the person who pays the tax to the tax collection authorities whereas the incidence of a tax is on the person who *bears* the tax. For example in the case of sales tax, sales tax is paid to tax authorities by the shop-keeper but borne by the consumer. We can say the impact of sales tax is on the shop-keeper but its incidence is on the consumer. In the case of income tax, the person who pays the tax is the wage earner. He is also the person who bears it as he cannot recover it from any body else. Thus the impact and incidence of income tax is on the same person. Income tax is therefore a Direct Tax. Other examples of direct taxes are corporation tax, estate duty, capital gains tax, etc.

Indirect Taxes

A tax is said to be indirect when its impact and incidence are on different persons. The impact of an indirect tax is either on an importer, manufacturer or a trader but the incidence is always on the final consumer. Indirect taxes are levied on goods and services and are of three main kinds, viz customs duties, excise duties and export duties.

1. *Customs Duties* are levied on goods imported from abroad.
2. *Excise Duties* are levied on goods and services produced within Kenya.
3. *Export Duties* are levied on goods exported from Kenya. At present Export Duty is levied on coffee and tea only.

Taxes on Income

These include Income Tax and Corporation Tax. Income tax is payable by individuals on their earnings whether in form of emoluments from employment, interest on investments, profit from business, professional fees, royalties, etc. Income Tax is progressive, i.e. its rate rises with income. For the year 1978 income tax rate is 10% on first £1,200, 15% on next £1,200, 25% on next £1,200 and gradually rises to 65% of the income. Profits made by joint stock companies are taxed by means of a Corporation Tax which at present is 45% of net profits.

Taxes on Capital

These include such taxes as estate duty, capital gains tax, etc. Estate duty is payable on the value of property that passes on death of a person to another person. Estate of a net capital value of £5,000 or less is at present exempt from this duty. Capital Gains tax was introduced in 1975 and is payable on capital gains accruing on the disposal of certain assets.

Taxes on Expenditure

These include customs and excise duties, sales tax, local rates, licence duties, etc. A person pays these taxes according to the volume of his expenditure, thus if he buys more goods liable to sales tax, he will pay more by way of sales tax.

THE BUDGET

The word 'budget' is derived from a Latin word 'bulga' meaning a bag. We may define a budget as a statement of estimated revenue and expenditure of a government for the coming financial year. Kenya government's financial year runs from 1st July to 30th June. On a certain day in June each year the Minister for Finance and Economic Planning presents the budget for approval of the parliament.

By the time the budget is introduced the estimate of expenditure under the various headings will have been presented to parliament and published in Kenya Gazette and the expected total of government expenditure for the coming year will be known. The Minister estimates the yield of the revenue on the basis of existing taxation and proposes such changes as he considers desirable on economic and other grounds. These proposals are embodied in detail in a Finance Bill.

INCOME TAX DEPARTMENT

This department falls under the jurisdiction of the Ministry of Finance and Economic Planning. Until December 1973, Income Tax Department was under the East African Community which administered income tax assessment and collection for all three partner states. With passing of the Income Tax Act (Cap. 470), the Kenya government assumed the responsibility of the administration of the department in 1974. The over-all conduct and running of the department is the responsibility of the Commissioner of Income Tax who is appointed by and is answerable to the Minister for Finance and Economic Planning.

The department carries out two major functions—to assess income tax and to collect it. Assessment of tax is carried out by five regional offices in Nairobi, Mombasa, Kisumu, Nakuru and Thika. Collection of tax is the responsibility of the Chief Collector of Income Tax whose offices are in Nairobi. Nairobi regional office has four districts as follows:

District 1—assesses tax on employees in private sector.
District 2—assesses tax on self-employed persons.
District 3—assesses tax on employees in government and parastatal bodies' employment.
District 4—assesses corporation tax on joint stock companies.

Each of the districts in Nairobi regional office is headed by a Principal Assessor of Income Tax. Mombasa office is also headed by a Principal Assessor of Income Tax whereas chief officers at other regional offices are senior assessors of income tax.

QUESTIONS

1. Discuss the necessity of levying taxes.
2. Discuss the principles of taxation. Do you think every citizen must contribute equally towards the expenditure of government? Give reasons for your answer.

3. Write short notes on the various types of taxes.
4. What is meant by (a) Incidence of Tax? (b) Impact of Tax?
5. Define a budget. In what respects, do you think, a government's budget differs from the budget of a commercial undertaking?
6. Write a short note on the organisation structure of the Kenya Income Tax Department.

Chapter Two

PERSONS LIABLE AND INCOME CHARGEABLE

INCOME TAX YEAR

The Income Tax Year in Kenya coincides with the calendar year. It is defined as 'the period of 12 months running from 1st January to 31st December of each year'. At the beginning of each year the Income Tax Department sends to all known taxpayers an *Income Tax Return Form* that incorporates a notice requiring the return to be completed to show income received by the taxpayer from all sources during the previous year. Thus Tax Return forms sent by the Income Tax Department in the beginning of 1977 should be completed to show all income earned in 1976. These forms should be returned to the Income Tax Department within 30 days. In exceptional cases a longer period may be allowed by the Tax Department where it may not be possible for a taxpayer to complete his returns within one month.

If a person liable to tax fails to receive the tax return form within four months after the end of an income tax year, he is required to notify the commissioner within 14 days after the expiry of four months that he has become liable to tax.

PERSONS LIABLE TO INCOME TAX

The liability to pay tax extends, in general, to:

(a) All persons resident in Kenya, whether or not they are Kenya citizens.
(b) All persons not resident in Kenya, whether or not Kenya citizens, in so far as they derive income from any property, trade, profession, vocation or employment in Kenya.

Income Tax is charged on income that accrues in or is derived from the partner states in East Africa. This principle applies to both residents and non-residents in Kenya. Income arising abroad, whether or not it is remitted to Kenya, is not liable to tax here. There is, however, one special exception to this rule. If a business is established in Kenya and has branches in foreign countries, profits made by its foreign branches would be taxed in Kenya.

RESIDENT

Residence is a matter of physical presence and a question of fact to be decided by the Commissioner of Income Tax. A person can have only one domicile but he may be 'resident' in several countries at the same time.

If an individual has permanent home in Kenya and was present in Kenya for any period in any particular year of income, he will be considered a resident of Kenya for that year of income. This rule, however, does not apply to him if he works full-time in a trade, profession or vocation no part of which is carried out in Kenya, or if he works full-time in an office or employment all the duties of which are performed outside Kenya.

If an individual has no permanent home in Kenya but was present in Kenya in any income tax year for a period or periods amounting in aggregate to 183 days (6 months) or more he will be considered as resident in Kenya in that income tax year. In addition, a person who does not stay in Kenya for more than six months in any income tax year but was actually in Kenya in a year and each of the two previous years for periods averaging more than 122 days (4 months), he will be regarded as a resident.

A body of persons, e.g. a joint stock company, will be considered as resident if:

(a)   the body is a company incorporated under a law of Kenya, or

(b)   the management and control of the affairs of the body is exercised in Kenya, or

(c)   the body has been declared by the Minister, by a notice in the Kenya Gazette, to be resident in Kenya for any year of income.

Any person whose residence circumstances do not come within this definition is considered a non-resident person.

INCOME CHARGEABLE TO TAX

The various forms of income chargeable to tax are as follows:

(a)   *Business Profits*

These include profit from any trade, profession or vocation.

(b)   *Employment or services rendered*

This includes wages, salaries, fees and pension arising from any office or employment.

(c) *Use of Property*

Profits or gains arising from rent or receipts from land or buildings. It also covers other payments related to the use of property such as key money or premium for a lease.

(d) *Dividends or Interests*

(e) *Any Pension or Annuity*

This includes payments made under pension schemes and provident funds.

(f) *Alimony or Allowance*

Received under a divorce decree or judicial order for separation or maintenance agreement.

(g) *Any amount deemed to be income*

This includes settlement made in favour of a child who is under 19 years of age—the income will be deemed to be of the settler and not of the child.

WIFE'S INCOME

Under Section 45 of the Income Tax Act, the income of a married woman living with her husband is deemed to be the income of the husband for the purpose of ascertaining his total income and he is required to account for the tax thereon.

If the husband fails to pay the tax, the tax can be collected from the wife or if she is dead, from her executors or administrators. The amount of tax to be collected from the wife will bear the same proportion to the total tax as her income bears to the total income of the husband.

Example 1: Income of Mr Njoroge   Shs. 36,000 in 1976
Income of Mrs Njoroge   Shs. 12,000 in 1976
Total Tax assessed (say)   Shs. 6,000 in 1976

If Mr Njoroge fails to pay tax relating to his wife's income, the amount of tax to be collected from her will be computed as follows:

$$\frac{\text{Income of wife}}{\text{Total Income}} \times \text{Total Tax Assessed.}$$

$$= \frac{12,000}{48,000} \times 6,000 = \text{Shs. } 1,500.$$

(Note: Total income means sum of incomes of both the husband and wife)

Income tax must be paid within 30 days of the date on which the Income Tax Department serves notice to a wife (or her executors or administrators) whose husband has failed to pay her tax.

If a married woman is not living with her husband then each of the spouses is treated as if he or she were unmarried.

A married woman is deemed to be living with her husband unless:

(a) They are separated under a court order, or under any written agreement of separation, or

(b) They are separated in such circumstances that the separation is likely to be permanent, or

(c) She is resident of Kenya and her husband is a non-resident, or vice versa.

INCOME OF INCAPACITATED PERSONS

The income of an incapacitated person is assessed in the name of his trustee, guardian, curator committee or receiver appointed by a court in such a manner as if he were not an incapacitated person.

INCOME OF NON-RESIDENT PERSONS

The income of a non-resident person is assessed in his name, or in the name of his trustee, guardian, curator committee, or his attorney, factor, agent, receiver or manager.

INCOME OF DECEASED PERSONS

The income accrued to or received prior to the date of death of a deceased person will be assessed on his executor or administrator. The law specifies that the assessment must be made within three years after the year in which the death occurs. Thus if a person dies in 1973, his income must be assessed before the end of 1976.

EXEMPTION FROM INCOME TAX

The Part I of the first schedule of the Income Tax Act 1973 specifies the incomes which are exempt from Kenya Income Tax. Some of them are as follows:

(1) That part of the income of the President of the Republic of Kenya that is derived from salary, duty allowance and entertainment allowance paid or payable to him from public

funds in respect of or by virtue of his office as the President of the Republic of Kenya.

(2)   The income of:

The Tea Board of Kenya
The Pyrethrum Board of Kenya
The Sisal Board of Kenya
The Canning Crops Board
The Kenya Dairy Board
The Central Agriculture Board
The Pig Industry Board
The Wheat Board
The Pineapple Development Authority
The Horticultural Crops Development Authority
The Kenya Tea Development Authority
The National Irrigation Board
The Mombasa Pipeline Board
etc.

(3)   The income of any co-operative society registered under the Co-operative Societies Act derived solely from selling on behalf of its members agricultural produce, dairy produce, the products of animal husbandry, handicrafts or fish. Other conditions are that the members of such a co-operative society must be primary producers and the gross income of each member should not exceed Shs. 3,000 per annum from such society.

(4)   The income, other than income from investment, of an amateur sporting association.

(5)   Profits or gains of an agricultural society accrued in or derived from Kenya from any exhibition or show held for the purpose of raising revenue for such an agricultural society, and interest on investment by such a society, e.g. A.S.K.

(6)   The income of any local authority.

(7)   Interest on any tax reserve certificate which may be issued by authority of the Government of Kenya.

(8)   The income of any registered pension scheme.

(9)   The income of any registered trust scheme.

(10) The income of any registered pension fund.

(11) The income of any registered provident fund.

(12) The income from the investment of an annuity fund, as defined in Section 19 of the Income Tax Act 1973, of an insurance company.

(13) Pension or gratuities granted in respect of wounds or disabilities caused in war and suffered by the recipients of such

pensions or gratuities.

(14) The income of any post office savings bank managed and controlled by the East African Posts and Telecommunications Corporation.

(15) Interest not exceeding Shs. 1,000 per annum from Post Office savings account to an individual (not company).

Part II of the first schedule of the Income Tax Act 1973 specifies the securities the interest on which is exempt from tax. It must be noted that the exemption is available only to non-resident persons. The securities are:

Kenya Government $2\frac{2}{3}$% stock 1977/83
Kenya Government 3½% stock 1973/78
Kenya Government 4½% stock 1971/78
Kenya Government 5% stock 1978/82
Kenya Government 5½% stock 1976/80
Kenya Government 6½% stock 1972/74
Kenya Government 6% Loan to finance Development Programme 1957/60, 1960/63 and 1980/93.

Nairobi City Council 3¼% stock 1970/74
East African High Commission 4% stock 1972/74
East African High Commission 4% stock 1973/76
East African High Commission 5½% stock 1980/84
East African High Commission 5% International Co-operation Administration Loan 1978
East African High Commission 4¾% International Bank for Reconstruction and Development Loans 1974 (two issues)
East African High Commission 5¾% stock 1977/83.

The above list is not conclusive and keeps on growing as Kenya Government issues fresh stock.

Any class of income which accrues in or is derived from Kenya can be declared exempt from tax if the Minister publishes a notice to this effect in the Kenya Gazette. Similarly by giving a notice in the Kenya Gazette the Minister can withdraw any exemption previously granted.

QUESTIONS

1. List the persons who are liable to tax in Kenya.
2. Briefly explain the difference between a resident person and a citizen person.
3. How would you determine the residential status of a joint stock

company?

4. List the various incomes that are chargeable to tax in Kenya.

5. How is the income of the following persons treated when computing income tax:
   (a)   an incapicitated person?
   (b)   a non-resident person?
   (c)   a married woman living with her husband?
   (d)   a married woman living separately from her husband?
   (e)   a deceased person?

6. With reference to the First Schedule of the Income Tax Act, list the various bodies whose income is exempt from income tax.

7. Under Kenya taxation laws the income of a married woman is considered a part of her husband's income, but in certain other countries it is possible for a married couple to have their incomes assessed separately. Discuss the comparative advantages, disadvantages and effects on the two methods of assessing income of married persons.

Chapter Three

RETURNS OF INCOME AND BOOKS OF ACCOUNTS

WHAT IS A RETURN?

By definition a Return is any document containing statistical information filled-in a pre-printed form sent to an office, particularly a government office. The Income Tax Department, in order to be able to assess tax and allow reliefs, etc., must obtain a lot of statistical information both from the earner and the payer. This is done by sending Return Forms to employees and employers, and to businessmen and self employed people who are required to complete them, attach documentary proof where available, and return them to the Tax Department within a specified period. For the sake of convenience in discussion we will divide the Returns in two groups: Returns filled-in by the taxpayers and Returns filled-in by those who *pay* or from whom a taxpayer earns his income. In the first group fall the following:

1. Return of Income by employed and self employed.
2. Return of Income received on account of other persons.
3. Return of income exempt from tax.
4. Return of Lodgers and inmates.

In the second group fall the following returns:

1. Returns as to salaries, pensions, gratuities, etc.
2. Returns as to fees, commissions, royalties, etc.
3. Returns as to rent paid.
4. Returns in relation to settlements.
5. Returns in relation to registered pension funds.
6. Returns of annuity contract benefits.
7. Returns of dividends paid by resident companies.
8. Returns of dividends paid or credited by building societies.
9. Returns of interest paid or credited by banks, etc.

RETURNS OF INCOME

Section 52 of the Income Tax Act stipulates that the Commissioner of Income Tax, by giving a notice in writing, may require any person to furnish him within a reasonable time (not less than

30 days) with a return of income for any year containing a full and true statement of income earned by such a person. In case of employed persons such a notice is usually sent in January each year, asking them to file a return for the preceding year. The case of businessmen is however a bit complicated. They are allowed to make a Provisional Return of Income within three months of the end of their financial year. Thus if the financial year of a trader runs from 1st April to 31st March each year, he will be required to make a return for year ended 31st March 1977 before 30th June 1977. Later, within nine months of the end of his financial year, he should make a formal return. This is dealt with in greater detail later in this chapter.

In the following cases, the Commissioner of Income Tax may ask for a return of income for any part of a year, before or after the year to which the income relates:

1. If the Commissioner of Income Tax has any reason to believe that the person concerned is about to leave Kenya.
2. In the case of the executors or administrators of a deceased person's will.
3. In the case of the liquidator of a resident company.

Where any business is carried on by two or more persons in partnership, the Commissioner may require precedent resident partner to complete a Return of Income of the partnership including names and addresses of all partners, together with the amount of the share of income to which each partner was entitled. For the purpose of Section 52 of the Income Tax Act a precedent resident partner is the one (a) whose name appears first in the Partnership Agreement, or (b) if there is no formal agreement of partnership, whose name appears first in the usual name of the partnership, or (c) if the partnership is not carried out in the names of the individual partners, whose name is usually written first in any statement required for the purposes of registration of business under any law of Kenya, or (d) whose name appears after the precedent resident partner if the precedent resident partner is not an active partner.

A person who fails to receive a notice to file a return of income within 4 months of the expiry of his year of income must inform the Commissioner, within 14 days of the expiry of the 4 months, that he has become chargeable. Thus in the case of an employed person, if he fails to get a notice by 30th April, he must inform the Commissioner of Tax before 15th May that he is chargeable to tax. There are however two exception to this procedure. In the case of businessmen the 4 months period begins from the end of his financial year, not necessarily the calendar year. Again an employed person is not required to notify the Commissioner of his failure to receive any notice to file a return of income if his entire income consists of emoluments from employment and the entire tax has been deducted at source by way of PAYE. This implies that if an employed person has any source of income in addition to the emoluments from employment, he must inform the Commissioner of Income Tax after 4 months have passed since the end of the year of income and he has not received the notice to file a return.

PENALTY

Any person who fails to furnish a return of income required by the Commissioner will be charged with additional tax equal to 5% of the normal tax for each period of 12 months or part thereof.

PROVISIONAL RETURNS OF INCOME

Certain businessmen cannot possibly ascertain their correct profit or loss for any financial year immediately after its end. Their books of accounts have to be balanced, and audited and financial statements drawn up—a procedure that must, of necessity, begin after the end of the financial year. It may take several months before they are able to produce an audited or certified statement of profit and loss and a balance sheet. Such businessmen are allowed to file a formal return of income within 9 months of the date of end of their financial year. They must however file a provisional return of income within three months of the end of their financial year. An employed person is not usually required to make a provisional return but may be asked to do so if he has a source of income other than emoluments from employment.

A provisional return should contain:
(a)   an estimate of the income based on all available information.
(b)   an estimate of tax chargeable on such estimated income.

Great care should be exercised when making these estimates as there is a provision in Income Tax Act that if the tax finally assessed is greater by 20% or more than the estimate of tax contained in the provisional return interest at the rate of 1% per month will be charged on the difference.

Any person who may be required to furnish a provisional return of income and who fails to receive a notice within four months of the end of his financial year must notify the Commissioner of Income Tax in writing within 14 days after the expiry of four months that he has not received a notice.

Documents to be Included in Return of Income Tax

Section 54 of the Income Tax Act specifies the following documents that should be included in returns of income.

1. Where a person carries on any business and if his accounts are prepared or examined by a professional accountant, his return of income should include:
   (a) A copy of his accounts signed by the accountant.
   (b) A certificate signed by the accountant stating:
       (i) the nature of books and documents from which the accounts were prepared, and
       (ii) whether he considers that such accounts present a true and fair view of the profits of the business.
   (c) In the case of a company or a partnership, a certificate specifying the nature and amount of all payments and benefits granted to the directors (or partners) and employees whose emoluments are at the rate of Shs. 40,000 per annum or more. Such a certificate should be signed by a majority of the directors (or partners), or if there are less than three directors or partners, by all the directors or partners.
2. The Commissioner of Income Tax may, by giving a notice in writing, require the professional accountant who has prepared or examined the accounts to state:
   (a) whether to the best of his knowledge and belief, the certificate given by him is true and correct.
   (b) the extent of his verification of books, etc. where the accounts were *prepared* by him.
   (c) the nature of books, documents, etc. produced to him and the extent of his examination thereof, where the accounts were *examined* by him.
3. Where a professional accountant refuses to give a certificate referred to in paras 1 and 2 above, he is required to give reasons for his refusal to the person making the return of income and such person should forward the statement to the Commissioner of Income Tax.
4. Where any person who carries on a business makes a return of income and his accounts are not prepared or approved by a professional accountant, he should enclose his accounts with his return to support the information given in the return. He

should also enclose the following:
- (a) A certificate signed by himself:
  - (i) specifying the nature of books and documents from which his accounts have been prepared.
  - (ii) stating whether his accounts give a true and fair view of the profits of the business.
- (b) Same as in para 1 (c) above.

BOOKS OF ACCOUNTS

Where a person chargeable with tax fails or refuses to keep books or accounts, the Commissioner of Income Tax has powers to require such a person to keep proper books and to keep them in such language as may be specified by the Commissioner.

PRESERVATION OF BOOKS AND ACCOUNTS

Every businessman is required to preserve all books of accounts and other accountancy records and documents for a period of not less than 10 years after the year of income to which such books and documents relate. There are however two exceptions to this requirement.
- (a) Books and documents need not be preserved if the Commissioner of Income Tax notifies the businessman in writing that their preservation is not required.
- (b) If a person who has custody of the books and documents of a company that has gone into liquidation and has been finally dissolved, or a person who holds records of a business other than a company that has ceased to exist, informs the Commissioner of Income Tax that he proposes to destroy the books and records, and if he fails to hear within three months of his notice to the Commissioner, he can destroy them.

RETURNS BY THOSE WHO PAY TAXPAYERS

The Commissioner of Income Tax may, by giving a notice in writing, require any employer, or any other person making a payment that may be considered a taxable income to the recepient, to furnish him, within a reasonable time (not less than 30 days) with any of the following returns.

1. *Return as to wages, salaries, etc.*

This return should give the following information:
- (a) The names and addresses of all persons to whom (or in respect of whom) payments of salaries and allowances,

including all benefits, advantages, etc. were made in respect of their employment. It should also state the amount of payments made to each person.

(b) The names and addresses of all persons to whom pensions were paid, and the amount of pension paid to each person.

2. *Return as to fees, commissions, royalties, etc.*

This return should give the following information:

(a) Name and address of each payee and the amount of payment made to him in the course of business for services rendered or to be rendered in future if such a payee is not employed by the business.

(b) Names, addresses and the amounts of payment made in connection with formation, acquisition, development or disposal of the business, or any part of it, by persons not employed by the business.

(c) Names, addresses and the amounts of periodical or lump sum payments in respect of any royalty made to any person.

3. *Return as to rent paid*

Every tenant is required to give the following information:

(a) The name and address of the owner, or lessor, of the premises occupied by him.

(b) A full and true statement of the rent and/or any other consideration payable for the occupation of premises.

4. *Return of Income received on account of other persons*

Any person who is in receipt of any income on behalf of other person(s) may be required to furnish a return containing a full and true statement of such income and the name and address of the person(s) to whom the income belongs.

5. *Return in relation to settlements*

Trustees will be required to give any information the commissioner of income tax may require in connection with any settlements.

6. *Return by registered pension funds*

The trustees of any registered pension fund or pension scheme and any employer who contributes to any such fund may be required to give the following information:

(a) The name and place of residence of every person in receipt of any amount under such scheme or fund.

(b) The amount and nature of payments.
(c) A copy of accounts of any such fund or scheme.
(d) Any further information that may be required by the Commissioner of Income Tax.

7. *Return of annuity contract benefits*

Any person by whom benefits are payable under any annuity contract may be required to give the full name and address of each person to whom any annuity has been paid by him, and the amount of such annuity.

8. *Return of resident company dividends*

Resident companies may be required to give the following information regarding dividends paid to shareholders:
(a) Full name and address of each shareholder and full particulars of his shareholding at the date when dividends were declared.
(b) The gross amount paid or payable and the tax deducted from such dividends.

9. *Return of dividends paid or credited by building societies*

Resident building societies give details similar to ones given by resident companies in respect of all shareholders, whether resident or non-resident. Foreign building societies in Kenya are, however, required to give details of dividends paid or credited to resident persons only, and also names and addresses of such persons.

10. *Return of interest paid or credited by banks, etc.*

Any person, or body, carrying on a business that in ordinary course of operations receives and retains money in such circumstances that interest becomes payable thereon may be required to give the following information:
(a) The names and addresses of the persons to whom the interest was paid or credited.
(b) The amount of interest paid or credited.

QUESTIONS

1. What is a return?
2. How often should a return of income be filed?
3. How does a provisional return of income differ from other returns of income?

4. List the contents of (a) a normal return of income, (b) a provisional return of income.
5. What documents, if any, must be attached with a return of income filed by:
   (a) an employed person,
   (b) a sole trader,
   (c) a partnership?
6. Discuss the provisions of the Income Tax Act regarding:
   (a) books of accounts.
   (b) preservation of books of accounts.
7. List the various returns that must be filed by those who pay taxpayers.

Chapter Four

CALCULATING TAX ON INCOME FROM EMPLOYMENT

GENERAL PROCEDURE

Computation of income tax usually involves the following stages:

1. Ascertaining gross income from all sources.
2. Deducting from gross income such amounts that may be allowable or such income that may not be taxable.
3. Ascertaining net income.
4. Calculating gross tax, using tax rates as applicable to the particular year of income.
5. Deducting from gross tax such reliefs that may be allowable.
6. Ascertaining net income tax for the year.
7. In the case of employed persons whose tax is deducted at source by way of P.A.Y.E. the amount of tax already deducted should be subtracted from the net income tax (Stage 6 above). The balance, if any, will be the amount still payable at the date of assessment.

ASCERTAINING GROSS INCOME

Section 5 subsection 1 (a) of the Income Tax Act specifies the bases on which an income is liable to income tax in Kenya. Briefly, these are as follows:

1. Any amount paid to a person who is a resident in Kenya, in respect of any services rendered by him, whether in or outside Kenya. This will also apply to such a person who was a resident of Kenya at the time of employment or when the services were rendered even if he ceases to be a Kenya resident at a later date.
2. Any amount paid to a non-resident person in respect of any employment with or services rendered to an employer who is resident in Kenya, or the permanent establishment in Kenya of an employer who is not a resident of Kenya.

The Income Tax Act includes the following items as part of income of an employed person:

1. Wages, salaries, leave pay, sick pay, payment in lieu of leave.
2. Fees, commission, bonus, gratuity.
3. Subsistence, travelling, entertainment or other allowance received in respect of employment or services rendered. These will however be deducted from an employee's income, for the purpose of calculating income tax, if the Commissioner of Income Tax is satisfied that they were incurred wholly and exclusively in the production of his income from the said employment and that these payments represent reimbursements of amounts expended by the employee.
4. Value of any benefit, advantage or facility of whatever nature granted in respect of employment or services rendered if it exceeds Shs. 1,000 in any one year of income.
5. Compensation for loss of office. This is explained later in this chapter.
6. Medical Expenses. Where an employer has a written plan or scheme or by practice provides free medical services to all his employees, the value of such medical services is a non-taxable benefit to full-time employees and whole-time service directors of a company. If there is no plan, or scheme, or if the free medical services are provided only to some of the employees, the payment of medical bills is a taxable cash payment and must be included in monthly pay in the month in which the payment is made.
7. Passages. When an employer himself pays for or reimburses the cost of tickets for passage, including leave passages, for his employee and his family, the value of the passage is a taxable benefit to the employee. There is however an exception to this rule. The passages for employee and his family will not be taxable if the following three conditions are satisfied:
   (a) The employee is recruited outside Kenya.
   (b) He is in Kenya solely for the purpose of serving his employer, and
   (c) He is not a Kenya citizen.
   Even in the above case, the amount should actually be spent on passages. If an employee is given any amount which he is free to save or spend on whatever passages he chooses and he does not have to account to the employer, the amount will be a taxable benefit.

8. Pension Funds. Amounts paid by an employer as his contribution to any approved provident fund or scheme is a non-taxable benefit to the employee.

9. Insurance premium paid by an employer for an insurance policy on the life of his employee for the benefit of such employee or any of his dependants is a taxable benefit and must be added to the employee's income for the purpose of calculating tax. Also see paragraph on 'insurance relief'.

10. Use of motor car for private purposes. If an employee working for an employer with whom he is not connected by shareholding, blood, marriage or other family ties, is provided with a motor car which is available to be used for private purposes, the following benefits will be chargeable to income tax:

Motor cars upto 1,500 c.c.	£200 p.a.
Motor cars from 1,501 to 1,750 c.c.	£300 p.a.
Motor cars from 1,751 to 2,000 c.c.	£400 p.a.
Motor cars of 2,000 and more c.c.	£600 p.a.

Thus an employee whose annual salary inclusive of benefits other than motor car is £3,000 p.a. and is provided with a 1,600 c.c. car for private purposes will be taxed at £3,300. In the case of directors, shareholders and relatives in privately controlled companies, and self employed tax-payers adjustment will be made for the full private use of business motor cars.

11. Housing benefits. If an employee is provided with a house, 15% of his annual salary will be added as housing benefit. However if the employee is required to pay a nominal rent for the house provided by the employer such rent will be deducted from the 15% to arrive at the net value of housing benefit. In the case where the actual rent is paid to an employee, the amount so paid will be added to the employee's income from the employment. Thus if an employee is paid an annual salary of £2,400 and is also paid an allowance for housing at the rate of £50 per month, he will be taxed at £3,000 (£2,400 plus £50 x 12).

ALLOWABLE DEDUCTIONS FROM INCOME

The following amounts may be deducted from gross earnings to arrive at chargeable income:

1. If an employee is provided with a house by his employer, 15% of his salary is added to salary as house allowance.

However from this additional 15% can be deducted the amount of rent charged by the employer. Thus if an employee earns £3,000 per annum and is provided with a house for which the employer deducts rent at the rate of Shs. 400 per month, his chargeable pay will be arrived at as follows:

	£
Basic Salary	3,000
Add 15% house allowance	450
Gross Salary	3,450
Less House Rent (£20 x 12)	240
Chargeable income	3,210

But if the rent charged by the employer is more than 15% of the salary, the excess is *not* deductible from basic salary. Thus if in the above example the rent charged by the employer was £50 per month, the rent for the year, £600, would be more than 15% of the salary, £450. In this case the chargeable pay will remain £3,000.

2. Pension upto a maximum of Shs. 50,000 per annum, or Shs. 4,160 per month is non-taxable. This should however, be added to other income earned by the taxpayer and tax calculated on the total amount. From the total tax, should be deducted the tax attributeable to pension, the balance being the tax for the year. Effect of this exercise is to put the other income received by a pensioner in a higher tax bracket. See on page 30 for further detail on this point.

3. If an employee uses a private machine, like a motor car, for the purpose of production of income from employment, he is allowed a capital deduction. In case of motor cars it is 25% of written down value.

4. If an employee pays any expenses for the purpose of production of income from his employment, and if such expenses are *not* reimbursed by his employer, these may be deducted from his gross earnings to arrive at his chargeable income.

Example 2:

M. Charo is a managing director of ABC Co. Ltd. He provides you with the following information about his earnings and expenses in 1977:

    (a)   Basic Salary, £4,200 per annum.

    (b)   He is provided with a house by the company for which

he pays a monthly rent of Shs. 1,000 to his employers.

(c) He is required to use his personal car for business purposes. In 1977 the cost of running his car amounted to Shs. 6,000. The cost of his car is Shs. 40,000. He estimates that three-fifths of use of his car is for business purposes.

(d) Total telephone bill for the year, Shs. 9,000. He estimates that two-third of the calls were made for business purposes.

His chargeable pay will be arrived as follows:

	£	£
Salary		4,200
Add: Housing @ 15% of £4,200	630	
Less Rent paid (£50 x 12)	600	
		30
Gross Pay		4,230
Less: Car Expenses (3/5ths of £300)	180	
Wear & Tear on car (3/5ths of 25% of £2,000)	300	
Telephone (2/3rds of £450)	300	
		780
Chargeable income		3,450

It should however be noted that if an employee incurs any expenses in order to be able to perform his duties, these expenses are *not* deductible from gross earnings. The expenses are deductible only if they are incurred when performing the duties. Thus if an employee travels every morning from his house to his place of work, the expenses related to these journeys are not allowable, but if he travels on business purpose from, say, his office to, say, to a client's office, any expenses related to this journey will be allowable. Thus if in the above example Mr Charo claimed any deduction for journeys made every morning from house to office, this will not be allowed.

CALCULATING GROSS INCOME TAX

Gross tax is calculated on net earnings, i.e. chargeable pay, according to the tax rates applicable to the particular year of income. Theoretically these rates may vary from year to year, but in practice the changes in tax rates are less frequent than that. Since Kenya took over the administration of the Income Tax Department in 1974, there has been only one change in rates in 1978. Given below are the tax rates, both old and the new effective from 1st January 1978.

Income Tax Rates for Years 1974, 1975, 1976 and 1977		*Income Tax Rates for Year 1978*	
On first £1,200	2/- per £	On first £1,200	2/- per £
On next £600	3/- per £	On next £1,200	3/- per £
On next £600	4/- per £	On next £1,200	5/- per £
On next £600	5/- per £	On next £1,200	7/- per £
On next £600	6/- per £	On next £1,200	9/- per £
On next £600	7/- per £	On next £1,200	10/- per £
On next £600	8/- per £	On next £2,400	12/- per £
On next £600	9/- per £	On any income over £9,600	13/- per £
On next £600	10/- per £		
On next £600	11/- per £		
On next £600	12/- per £		
On next £1,800	13/- per £		
On any income over £9,000	14/- per £		

Example 3:

Mr Mburu's chargeable pay for years 1977 and 1978 was £3,240 p.a. Calculate his gross tax for the two years:

Year 1977:	Shs.
On £1,200 @ 2/- per £	2,400
On £600 @ 3/- per £	1,800
On £600 @ 4/- per £	2,400
On £600 @ 5/- per £	3,000
On £240 @ 6/- per £	1,440
Gross Tax for 1977	11,040

Year 1978:	
On £1,200 @ 2/- per £	2,400
On £1,200 @ 3/- per £	3,600
On £840 @ 5/- per £	4,200
Gross Tax for 1978	10,200

RELIEFS DEDUCTIBLE FROM GROSS INCOME TAX

A Relief is an amount that can be deducted from gross income tax to arrive at net income tax. Net income tax is the amount for which an employed person is liable. Distinction must be made between an 'allowance' deductible from gross earnings to arrive at chargeable income and a 'relief' deductible from gross income tax to arrive at net income tax.

Example 4:

Mr Kimani earns an annual salary of £2,800 but is required to use his personal car for business purposes. He is married. During 1978 he incurred the following expenses:

(a)   Running and maintenance of car, £500. He estimates that 60% of the total use of car was for business purposes.

(b)   Wear and tear, at 25% of the written down value of car, £450.

He was not refunded any expenses.

His tax liability will be calculated as follows:

	£	£
Salary		2,800
Less: Running & Maintenance of		
Car, 60% of £500	300	
Wear and Tear, 60% of £450	270	
		570
Chargeable income		2,230

	Shs.
Tax on £1,200 @ 2/- per £	2,400
£1,030 @ 3/- per £	3,090
Gross Income Tax	5,490
Less: Family Relief	1,680
Net Income Tax for 1978	3,810

Notes: (1)   In the above example, the sum of £570 that was deducted from Mr Kimani's gross pay is an *allowance*. And the sum of Shs. 1,680 (Family Relief) that was deducted from his gross income tax is a *relief.*

(2)   The amount of Shs. 3,810 shown as net income tax is the total amount for the year. From this amount must be deducted any P.A.Y.E. that may already have been deducted by Mr Kimani's employers.

The following reliefs are at present permissible to individual tax-payers in Kenya:

1. *Single Relief*

   For the years 1974 to 1977 Single Relief was Shs. 360 per annum, or Shs. 30 per month. In 1978 the Single Relief has been raised to Shs. 600 per annum, or Shs. 50 per month. Single Relief may be claimed by a person who is unmarried, widower, divorcee, or legally separated from his/her spouse. From 1978 onwards a distinction is kept between a single person with one or more children who is entitled to Special Single Relief.

2. *Special Single Relief*

   This relief has been introduced in 1977/78 budget but is effective from January 1978. It is allowed to a single person who maintains one or more children. It amounts to Shs. 720 per annum, or Shs. 60 per month.

   This relief is available only if the taxpayer proves that at the commencement of the year he maintained any child of his:

   (a) who was under the age of 18 years on that date and who was either in his custody, or any other person's custody by virtue of an order of a competent court, or

   (b) who was above 18 years of age but was:
        (i)   receiving full-time education, or
        (ii) serving full-time articles or indentures, or
        (iii) totally incapacitated either mentally, or physically from maintaining himself and was resident in Kenya, or in a recognized institution abroad.

   (c) whose income (child's income) does not exceed Shs. 1,800 in any one year.

   A person cannot claim both the single and special single relief at the same time.

3. *Married Relief*

   For the purpose of calculating income tax, a wife's earnings are added to her husband's earnings and income tax is calculated on the total so derived. From the tax calculated on their total earnings a Married Relief is deducted. For the years 1974 to 1977 this relief was Shs. 720 per annum, or Shs. 60 per month. This relief has been abolished in 1978 and replaced by a Family Relief.

4. *Child Relief*

   In years 1974 to 1977 a child relief was allowed at Shs. 180

per child per annum for upto a maximum of 4 children. This relief has been abolished from 1978. However, its abolition has been more than compensated for by introduction of special single and family reliefs.

5. *Family Relief*

This relief has been introduced with effect from January 1978 and is available to any couple who were married before 1st January 1978. It amounts to Shs. 1,680 per annum, or Shs. 140 per month. It is available to married persons whether or not they have any children.

Family Relief is usually claimed by the husband and full tax is deducted from the wife's salary.

6. *Insurance Relief*

This relief is available to a resident individual if:
(a) he has paid a premium for an insurance policy on his own life or on the life of his wife.
(b) the insurance policy secures a capital sum on death, whether or not in conjunction with other benefits.
(c) the policy is taken out from an insurance company carrying on lawfully the business of life insurance in Kenya.
(d) any sums payable under the policy are payable in Kenya in Kenya currency.

This relief is available to an employed person if he pays the premium himself or if his employer pays it for him. In the latter case any payment made by the employer would be treated as a taxable benefit to the employee and added to his (employee's) income.

The rate of this relief is 2/- per £ and the maximum relief is Shs. 480 per annum. In years 1974 to 1977 this relief was Shs. 360 per annum. The increase from Shs. 360 to Shs. 480 per annum became effective from 1st January 1978.

Example 5:

Mr Omondi's gross earnings for 1978 amounted to £2,600. He is married and has an insurance policy for which he pays an annual premium of Shs. 3,000. Calculate his tax liability for 1978.

	Shs.
Tax on £1,200 @ 2/- per £	2,400
£1,200 @ 3/- per £	3,600
£200 @ 5/- per £	1,000
Gross Tax	7,000

	Shs.	Shs.
Less: Family Relief	1,680	
Insurance Relief		
@ 2/- per £ on £150	300	1,980
Net Tax for 1978		5,020

Example 6:

Mr Kendogar earns £3,200 in 1978. He is single and has an insurance policy for which he pays an annual premium of Shs. 5,600. Calculate his tax liability for 1978.

	Shs.
Tax on £1,200 @ 2/- per £	2,400
£1,200 @ 3/- per £	3,600
£800 @ 5/- per £	4,000
Gross Tax	10,000

	Shs.	
Less: Single Relief	600	
Insurance Relief		
@ 2/- per £ on £240	480	1,080
		8,920

Note: Mr Kendogar's insurance premium was £280 for 1978 but as the maximum relief is Shs. 480, he cannot be allowed a full relief of Shs. 560 on his premiums.

Pension Relief

This relief has rather a special nature. As stated earlier in this chapter, pension of upto Shs. 50,000 per annum is free of tax, but must first be added to other income(s) made by its recepient, tax calculated on total income, and from gross tax may be deducted the tax attributable to pension, to arrive at net tax.

Example 7:

Mr Jahazi receives an annual pension of Shs. 30,000. He is also employed and earns an annual salary of Shs. 36,000. He is married. Calculate his tax liability for 1978.

	£
Salary (Shs. 36,000)	1,800
Pension (Shs. 30,000)	1,500
Gross Income (in this case, also chargeable income)	3,300

		Shs.
Income Tax on £1,200 @ 2/- per £		2,400
£1,200 @ 3/- per £		3,600
£900 @ 5/- per £		4,500
Gross Tax		10,500

		Shs.	
Less: Family Relief		1,680	
Tax on Pension	Shs.		
on £1,200 @ 2/-	2,400		
on £300 @ 3/-	900		
		3,300	
			4,980
Net Tax for 1978			5,520

Example 8:

Mr Chepkwony has an annual pension of Shs. 60,000. He also draws an annual salary of Shs. 24,000. Calculate his tax liability for 1978 assuming that he is a widower.

	£
Salary (Shs. 24,000)	1,200
Pension (Shs. 60,000)	3,000
Chargeable Income	4,200

		Shs.
Income Tax on £1,200 @ 2/-		2,400
£1,200 @ 3/-		3,600
£1,200 @ 5/-		6,000
£600 @ 7/-		4,200
Gross Tax		16,200

		Shs.	
Less: Single Relief		600	
Tax attributeable to pension	Shs.		
on £1,200 @ 2/-	2,400		
on £1,200 @ 3/-	3,600		
on £100 @ 5/-	500		
		6,500	
			7,100
			9,100

Note: As maximum amount allowable for pension is Shs. 50,000 (or £2,500) per annum, tax attributeable to this amount only has been deducted as tax relief, though Mr Chepkwony's pension was in fact £3,000.

It will be observed from the above two examples that pension, though free of tax itself, puts other income in a higher tax bracket. Students are advised to calculate tax on the above two examples *without* including pension and see the difference in tax liability that results.

TREATMENT OF COMPENSATION FOR LOSS OF OFFICE

Any amount received as compensation for termination of any contract of employment or services is taxable whether or not provision is made in the employment contract for the payment of such compensation. The liability of tax is determined as follows:

(a)   A director of any company which is controlled by its directors, other than a whole-time service director, is assessable on all of the compensation in the year (or years) it accrued or was received. Thus if Mr Ndegwa is a director of a company that is controlled by its directors, and if Mr Ndegwa is not a whole-time director and he is paid a compensation of, say, £4,000, for loss of office in 1978, the whole of £4,000 would be added to any other income(s) earned by him in 1978 and he would be taxed on the total so derived.

(b)   The liability to tax of employees and whole-time service directors is reduced as follows:

(1)   Contract for a specific term of service. If an employee is hired for a specific period but his services are terminated before the expiry of such period, the amount of compensation that is taxable is equal to the income that would have accrued to the employee in the unexpired period. Any amount paid in excess of this would be tax free.

Example 9:

Mr Biridi, the managing director of White Ice Ltd. was employed under a contract for five years ending 30th June 1978. His salary was £2,400. His contract was terminated on 31st December 1976 and he was paid a sum of £5,000 as compensation for loss of office.

Mr Biridi would have earned £3,600 during the unexpired period of contract, i.e. £2,400 in 1977 and £1,200 in 1978. The excess of £5,000 (amount of compensation) over £3,600 (salary for unexpired period), i.e. £1,400 would be tax-free. £2,400 would be added to any income that he may make in 1977, and £1,200 to income of 1978.

   (2)   Contract for unspecified term providing for compensation. In this case the amount of compensation is assessable in the years following the termination of contract at a rate of salary per annum applying on the date of cessation of contract.

Example 10:

Mr Moto, accountant to Fireworks Ltd., was hired without any contract for specific period. He drew a salary of £3,200 in 1977. His services were terminated on 31st December 1977 and he was paid a sum of £6,900 as compensation for loss of service.

He will be assessed at £3,200 in 1978, at £3,200 in 1979 and at £500 in 1980.

   (3)   Contract for unspecified term not providing for compensation. In this case the amount of compensation is taxed only during the three years following the termination of contract, at an annual rate of salary drawn by the employee in the year of termination. Any amount paid in excess of equavalent of three years salary is tax-free.

Example 11:

Mr Ngumu, general manager of Hardjob Ltd., drew an annual salary of £3,000 in 1976. His services were terminated on 31st December 1976 and he was paid £10,000 as compensation.

Mr Ngumu would be taxed on £3,000 in 1977, 1978 and 1979. The excess of £1,000 (£10,000 - £9,000) would be tax free.

Example 12:

Facts as for the above example, but this time we assume that he was paid only £8,000 as compensation.

He would be taxed on £3,000 in 1977 and 1978 and on £2,000 in 1979.

Treatment of settlement made in favour of a child

If a person settles any income in favour of his child, such income is considered as income of the settlor, unless it is less than Shs. 100 per annum, or the child is over 19 years of age.

Example 13:

Mr Mzee Kubwa settles an income of Shs. 3,000 per annum in favour of his child. His total income is Shs. 60,000 per annum.

In this case Mr Mzee Kubwa would be taxed on his total income of Shs. 60,000, not Shs. 57,000, even if Shs. 3,000 is not received by him but by his child.

QUESTIONS

1. Describe the general procedure for computation of income tax on the emoluments of an employed person.
2. Explain the difference between an allowance and a relief.
3. List the usual allowances available to an employed person.
4. List the usual reliefs available to an employed person.
5. In what respect is pension relief different from any other tax relief?
6. John Gathuru is employed as a clerk by a trading company. In 1978 he earned a total salary of Shs. 25,000. He was not provided with a house or a house allowance. He is single. Compute his net tax liability for 1978.
7. John Mbooni is employed as a clerk by a trading company. In 1978 his emoluments were as follows:

	£
Basic pay	900
House Allowance	300
Travelling Allowance	120

He is married with nine children. He also has an insurance policy on which he pays an annual premium of Shs. 1,200. Compute his net tax liability.

8. Omar Swaleh earned £2,400 from his employment in 1978. During the same year he earned £1,200 by way of insurance commission. His employer provides him with a house for which he pays a monthly rent of Shs. 200. He is married but has no children. He pays the following insurance premiums each year:
   (a) Shs. 2,500 on a policy on his own life.
   (b) Shs. 2,000 on a policy on his wife's life.
   (c) Shs. 1,000 on a policy on his house.
   Compute his net tax liability for 1978.
9. Zaid Bin Bakar is married with three children. He is employed as a salesman and is required to use his personal car

for official purposes for which he is not paid any special allowance. His earnings in 1978 were as follows:

	£
Basic salary	3,100
Commission	4,200
House Allowance	1,200

He estimates that he spent a total of £600 on his car for petrol, maintenance, and depreciation, etc. and that 75% of the use of car was for business purposes. He pays the following insurance premium each year:

	Shs.
On his own life policy	4,500
On his wife's life policy	2,000
On his children's education policy	2,000

Compute his net tax liability for 1978.

10. Given below are the details of income, etc. of three employed persons for 1978:

	Mbaya	Mburu	Mbuni
	£	£	£
Gross Pay	1,200	2,300	3,100
House Allowance	480	Nil	Nil
Housing Provided	No	Yes	Yes
House Rent charged by Employer	Nil	120 p.a.	600 p.a.
Marital Status	Single	Single	Married
No. of children maintained	Nil	Two	Three
Insurance Premium Paid on			
own life	Nil	200 p.a.	500 p.a.
wife's life	Nil	Nil	100 p.a.
children's life	Nil	50 p.a.	Nil
Pension Received	700	Nil	3,000
Travelling Allowance Received	Nil	240	Nil

Compute the net tax liability of the above persons for 1978.

11. Joseph Mugo, a single person with no children, receives a monthly salary of Shs. 2,000 and a house allowance of Shs. 400. He pays the whole of his house allowance to his landlord as rent for the flat occupied by him. One of the flats belonging to his employer has become vacant and he has been asked if he would like to occupy it. He would be required to pay a rent of Shs. 230 to his employer, including Shs. 25 for water and Shs. 30 for the use of furniture. He will cease to receive house allowance if he occupies the flat offered by the employer. Advise him.

12. Given below are the details of income, etc. of two employed

persons for the year 1978:

	Ndoria £	Ngandu £
Basic Pay	2,200	1,000
Housing Provided by Employer	Yes	No
Rent paid to Employer	300	Nil
Pension Received	1,200	2,600
Travelling & Other Allowances	900	Nil
Private Car:		
Maintenance and Other Expenses	500	480
Use for official purposes	100%	60% of total use
Marital Status	Widower	Widower
Number of Children	3, all over 18 years of age and working.	4, two at school, two working.
Insurance Premium on own life policy	Nil	200

Compute the net tax liability of the above persons for 1978.

13. Habel Gatama, the chief accountant of Power Industries Ltd., was employed on a five years contract on 1st January 1975 at an annual salary of £3,000. His services were terminated on 1st July 1978 and he was paid a sum of £6,200 as compensation for loss of office. Assuming that he does not take up any employment in the years 1978, 1979 and 1980, calculate his tax liability for these years.

14. Facts as for the above problems. Now assume that Mr Habel Gatama's contract was in fact for seven years and calculate his tax liability for the years 1978, 1979 and 1980.

15. Facts as for Problem 13. Now assume that Mr Gatama's contract was not for a fixed term but provided £6,200 as amount payable as compensation on termination. Calculate his tax liability for the years 1978, 1979 and 1980.

16. Facts as for Problem 13. Now assume that Mr Gatama's contract was not for a fixed term and that there was no specific provision in the contract for payment of compensation on termination. He was however paid the compensation of £9,200. Calculate his tax liability for the years 1978, 1979 and 1980.

Chapter Five

OPERATION OF P.A.Y.E.

EMPLOYERS' DUTY TO DEDUCT TAX

It is every employer's statutory duty to deduct income tax from the pay of his employees whether or not he has been specifically told to do so by the Income Tax Department.

If an employer fails to deduct tax from the emoluments paid to his employees, the Commissioner of Income Tax has the powers to impose a penalty not exceeding Shs. 4,000 and to require him to pay the tax which he should have deducted from his employees' income.

ESSENTIAL FEATURES OF P.A.Y.E.

(a) Every month when an employer pays salaries to his employees, he deducts tax on them according to tax rates applicable to the year of income. For all employed persons year of income runs from 1st January to 31st December.

(b) To pay the tax so deducted to the Income Tax Department before the 10th of the month following the deduction. Thus deductions made from June salaries (assuming these were paid on the last day, or before, of June) must be paid in by 10th July.

(c) A Tax Deduction Card is maintained for every employee on which the details of gross pay, housing, chargeable pay, gross tax, personal reliefs, and tax deducted, etc. are given.

(d) At the end of an income year all tax deduction cards are returned to the Income Tax Department.

TAX DEDUCTION CARD

This form is supplied to the employer by the Income Tax Department and one must be prepared for every employee liable to tax. The department is usually willing to allow an employer to use his own card or form so long as it shows the same information as the one issued by the department and the proposed design of the form is approved by the Commissioner of Income Tax. Government ministries, in particular, do not use the form supplied by the tax department but have their own forms which are maintained by computers.

How to make entries on a Tax Deduction Card

A Tax Deduction Card has the following columns:
  (a)   Pay for the month in shillings.
  (b)   Pay for the month in pounds, rounded to nearest pound.
  (c)   Housing in pounds.
  (d)   Chargeable pay for the month in pounds, i.e. (b) + (c).
  (e)   Tax Chargeable (or gross tax) in shillings.
  (f)   Monthly Personal Tax Relief in shillings.
  (g)   Unused Tax Relief in Shillings.
  (h)   Tax deducted in shillings.
The use of columns is explained below:
  (a)   In this column is entered the pay earned by an employee,
        expressed in shillings. Pay would include the salary and
        any cash allowance paid to the employee, e.g. house rent,
        house to office mileage allowance, etc.
  (b)   Pay listed in column (a) is converted to nearest £ and
        entered in column (b).
  (c)   If housing is provided by the employer, column (c) is
        used to record the excess of 15% of pay over the rent
        charged by the employer. Entries in column (c) are made
        in terms of nearest £. Amount to be entered is calculated
        as follows:
        Step 1 Calculate 15% of the amount entered in column
                (a) or (b).
        Step 2 From this amount deduct the rent charged to em-
                ployee.
        Step 3 Enter the balance in column (c).
  Note: If, however, rent charged by the employer is more than
          15% of the employee's salary, no figure should be re-
          corded in column (c). As explained in Chapter Four,
          the excess of rent charged to employee over 15% of
          his salary is not to be deducted from monthly pay.

Example 14:

   Column (a), Shs. 2,000.
   Rent paid by employee to employer, Shs. 100 per month.
   Entries to be made in columns (b) and (c) will be:

                                                              £
            Column (b), £100.
            Column (c) = 15% of £100 =   15
                       Less rent paid   5
                                                 ___
            Entry in Column (c)   10
                                                 ===

Column (a), Shs. 1,600.
Rent paid by the employee, Shs. 300 per month.
Entry in Column (b) = £80.

	£
15% of £80	12
Less rent paid by employee	15
Entry in Column (c)	NIL

Note: Rent paid by employee should be exclusive of any amounts paid for furniture, water, conservancy, electricity, etc. For example if an employee is provided with a furnished house for which he pays Shs. 400 per month, including Shs. 100 for furniture and Shs. 50 for water and conservancy, for tax purposes the rent paid by him will be taken as Shs. 250 (Shs. 400 less Shs. 100 less Shs. 50).

If housing is not provided by the employer, no entry is made in column (c), whether or not a housing allowance is paid. If a housing allowance is paid it is added on basic pay, and the total entered in column (a).

(d) In column (d) enter the total of columns (b) and (c). This represents the chargeable pay, in pounds, for the month.

(e) Using the tax tables, calculate the amount of tax on the figure entered in column (d). The amount to tax so calculated should be entered in column (e).

(f) Enter the amount of monthly personal relief in column (f). This amount is also shown on the top of Tax Deduction Card. As from 1st January 1974 the amount of MPR cannot be altered during the year. Thus if a person is entitled to single relief in January and gets married in February, he will not become entitled to family relief until January of the following year.

(g) Deduct the amount shown in column (f) from the amount shown in column (e). If the amount shown in column (f) is more than the amount shown in column (e), the amount represents unused MPR and should be entered in column (g). This can be carried forward to next month, but any unused MPR at the end of the year cannot be taken forward to next year.

(h) If the amount shown in column (e) is more than the amount shown in column (f), the difference must be entered in column (h). This amount represents the tax that should be deducted from the employee's salary and remitted to the Income Tax Department.

Example 15:

Mr Kadenge works as a salesman for Kenya Chai Co. Ltd. His income for the first four months of 1978 was as follows:

January, Shs. 1,800
February, Shs. 600
March, Shs. 1,900
April, Shs. 1,700

He is provided with a house by his employer for which a rent of Shs. 200 per month is deducted. He is married. Show the Tax Deduction Card entries for each of the four months.

Preliminary Calculations

January: Salary rounded to £ amounts to £90.
           Housing @ 15% of £90 comes to £13 (nearest £).
           Rent paid by Mr Kadenge is £10, thus amount to be entered in column (c) would be £13 - 10 = £3.
           Chargeable pay for the month amounts to £93. (£90 + 3).
           Tax on £93 @ 2/- per £ amounts to Shs. 186.
           MPR for a married person is Shs. 140 (Shs. 1,680 ÷ 12).
           Tax to be deducted should be Shs. 186 - 140 = 46.

February: Salary rounded to £ amounts to £30.
           Housing @ 15% of £30 comes to £4.50 which is less than rent paid by Mr Kadenge (£10). Hence, no entry in column (c).
           Chargeable pay for the month amounts to £30.
           Tax on £30 @ 2/- per £ amounts to Shs. 60.
           MPR for the month is Shs. 140, leaving an unused MPR of Shs. 80 which must be entered in column (g).
           No entry to be made in column (h) as no tax is deductible for this month.

March: Salary rounded to £ amounts to £95.
           Housing at 15% of £95 comes to £14.
           Rent paid is £10, thus amount to be entered in column (c) is £4 (£14 - 10).
           Chargeable pay for the month comes to £99 (£95 + 4).
           Tax on £99 at 2/- per £ comes to Shs. 198.
           MPR for the month is Shs. 140, but there is unused

MPR brought forward from February of Shs. 80. This gives a total of Shs. 220 which exceeds tax for the month (Shs. 198) by 22/-. Shs. 22 is thus unused MPR to be carried forward to April.

No entry to be made in column (h), as no tax is to be deducted in March.

April: Salary rounded to £ amounts to £85.

Housing at 15% of £85 comes to £13.

Rent paid is £10, thus amount to be entered in column (c) is £3.

Chargeable pay for the month comes to £88.

Tax on £88 at 2/- per £ comes to Shs. 176.

MPR for the month is Shs. 140, but there is unused MPR brought forward from March of Shs. 22. This gives a total of Shs. 162. Shs. 162 deducted from Shs. 176 gives a tax deductible figure of Shs. 14 which must be entered in column (h).

Now prepare the Tax Deduction Card as follows:

Tax Deduction Card

Month	(a)	(b)	(c)	(d)	(e)	(f)	(g)	(h)
	Shs.	£	£	£	Shs.	Shs.	Shs.	Shs.
January	1,800	90	3	93	186	140	—	46
February	600	30	Nil	30	60	140	c/f 80	Nil
March	1,900	95	4	99	198	140	used 80	Nil
							c/f 22	
April	1,700	85	3	88	176	140	used 22	14

Students are advised to try to complete an actual Tax Deduction Card, copies of which may be obtained on request from an Income Tax Office. Before surrendering Tax Deduction Cards at the end of year to the Tax Department an employer must total all its columns.

PROCEDURE ON LUMP SUM PAYMENTS

Before an employer makes any lump sum payment to any employee (e.g. gratuity, bonus, etc.), he must notify the Income Tax Department on appropriate forms, as follows:

(a) Lump sum payment to employee leaving Kenya permanently—on Form I.T. 390.

(b) Lump sum payment to employee proceeding on overseas leave but returning to Kenya—on Form I.T. 391.

REPUBLIC OF KENYA—INCOME TAX DEPARTMENT
TAX DEDUCTION CARD YEAR 19____

EMPLOYER'S NAME: Kenya Chai Co Ltd   EMPLOYER'S I.T. No. 38434773
EMPLOYEE'S MAIN NAME: KADENGE   PAY ROLL No. 518
EMPLOYEE'S OTHER NAMES: John   EMPLOYEE'S I.T. No. 38434773/518

Monthly Personal Relief		Original Sh. 140		Revised Sh.		Revised Sh.			Information Required from Employer at end of Year
Dates of Changes									(1) Date Commenced if During Year ____
	a	b	c	d	e	f	g		h	
Month	Pay of Month	Round Down to	Housing	Chargeable Pay of Month (b+c)	Tax Charged	Monthly Personal Relief	Record of Unused Relief		Tax Deducted	Name and Address of old Employer ____
	Sh.	£	£	£	Sh.	Sh.		Sh.	Sh.	
January	1800	90	3	93	186	140	Unused	-	46	____
February	600	30	NIL	30	60	140	C/Fwd 80 / Used Unused		NIL	(2) Date left if during Year:
March	1900	95	4	99	198	140	C/Fwd / Used Unused	80 22	NIL	Name and Address of new Employer ____
April	1700	85	3	88	176	140	C/Fwd / Used Unused	22	14	____
May	2000	100	5	105	215	140	C/Fwd / Used Unused		75	(3) Did Employee receive any benefits other than in cash totalling more than £50 in Year. If so state Amounts: £ NIL
June	2000	100	5	105	215	140	C/Fwd / Used Unused		75	
July	2000	100	5	105	215	140	C/Fwd / Used Unused		75	(4) Where housing is provided state Monthly rent charged: Sh. 200 Per Month
August	2000	100	5	105	215	140	C/Fwd / Used Unused		75	
September	2000	100	5	105	215	140	C/Fwd / Used Unused		75	(5) Where any of the Pay relates to a period other than this year, e.g. gratuity, give details of Amounts Year and Total
October	2000	100	5	105	215	140	C/Fwd / Used Unused		75	
November	2000	100	5	105	215	140	C/Fwd / Used Unused		75	Year / Amount £ / Tax Sh.
December	2000	100	5	105	215	140	C/Fwd / Used Unused		75	19 / /
TOTALS		1100	50	1150	2340	1680			660	19 / /

To be completed by Employer at end of year
Total Chargeable Pay (Col. d) £ 1150   Tax (Col. h) Sh. 660

	For Official use	Sh.
	Tax Due	
	Over Paid	
	Under Paid	

P9

GPK (L)

  (c)   Lump sum payment to employee leaving the employment permanently, even if remaining in Kenya—on Form I.T. 392.

On receipt of the above form(s), Income Tax Department calculates tax to be deducted from the lump sum payment and inform the employer on Form I.T. 393.

  (d)   When making a lump sum payment to an employee who is remaining in the same employment, the employer, instead of notifying the Income Tax Department, may calculate the tax on lump sum as follows:

      (1)   Calculate the tax for the whole year on the income from that employment, *including* the lump sum.

      (2)   Calculate the tax for the whole year on the income from that employment, *excluding* the lump sum.

      (3)   The difference between (1) and (2) above will be the tax on the lump sum payment.

Example 16:

Mr Hamisi is employed by Maji Moto Ltd. His monthly salary is Shs. 5,000. He is also provided with a house for which he pays a rent of Shs. 500 per month to his employer. In the month of July 1978 he was given a bonus of Shs. 18,000. Mr Hamisi is married and has taken out a life insurance policy on his own life for which he pays a premium of Shs. 2,400 per annum. Calculate the tax on lump sum and the amount of tax to be deducted from his pay in July 1978:

Step 1: Mr Hamisi's annual salary *with* bonus:

    Shs. 5,000 x 12 plus Shs. 18,000 = Shs. 78,000.
    Rounded to £, it amounts to £3,900.

	£
Housing @ 15% of £3,900	585
Less Rent paid by him	300
	285

    Chargeable income for the year = £3,900 plus £285 = £4,185.

Step 2: Tax on £4,185 (i.e. annual pay including bonus) will be calculated as follows:

	Shs.
on £1,200 @ 2/- per £	2,400
on £1,200 @ 3/- per £	3,600
on £1,200 @ 5/- per £	6,000
on £585 @ 7/- per £	4,095
on £4,185 tax before relief	16,095

Step 3: Mr Hamisi's annual salary *without* bonus:

Shs. 5,000 x 12 = Shs. 60,000 or £3,000.

	£
Housing @ 15% on £3,000	450
Less Rent paid by him	300
	150

Chargeable income = £3,000 + 150 = £3,150.

Step 4: Tax on £3,150 (i.e. annual pay excluding bonus) will be calculated as follows:

	Shs.
on £1,200 @ 2/- per £	2,400
on £1,200 @ 3/- per £	3,600
on £750 @ 5/- per £	3,750
on £3,150 tax before relief	9,750

Step 5: Tax on bonus will be calculated as follows:

	Shs.
Tax on pay including bonus (£4,185)	16,095
Tax on pay excluding bonus (£3,150)	9,750
	6,345

Step 6: Mr Hamisi's tax on July pay will be calculated as follows:

	£	£
Hamisi's pay for July		250
Housing @ 15% of £250	38	
Less Rent paid by him	25	13
Chargeable pay		263

	Shs.
Tax on £100 @ 2/- per £	200
on £100 @ 3/- per £	300
on £ 63 @ 5/- per £	315
Tax on £263 before relief	815

Less: Family Relief	Shs. 140	
Insurance Relief @ 2/- per £ on £10	Shs. 20	160

Tax for July pay	655
Add Tax on bonus as calculated above	6,345
Tax to be deducted in July	7,000

HUSBAND AND WIFE

The income of a married woman living with her husband is regarded as that of her husband for the purpose of calculating tax. The husband is responsible for completing the income tax return where he must give details of the couple's combined incomes. Additionally, the burden of satisfying any tax assessments falls on the husband's shoulders, and any claim for repayment of tax are made by, and the recoveries paid to, him.

No family relief is given to the husband in the year in which the marriage takes place. Husband and wife are treated as single persons and given single relief (i.e. Shs. 600) in the year of marriage. They fill-in separate tax returns for that year. Family tax relief is given in the next year from 1st January. This exercise is in accordance with the laid down policy of the Income Tax Department that there will be no change in tax relief during any year.

From the year following the year of marriage the husband is given a family relief which is deducted from his gross tax for the month (or year) but the wife's gross tax is deducted, i.e. she is not given any relief. There is a provision in the Act that should the husband and wife decide to apportion the tax relief they are allowed to do so. This is however not the general practice.

Example 17:

Kariuki and Wambui are husband and wife who live together. Kariuki's monthly salary in 1978 was Shs. 3,400 and Wambui's was Shs. 2,200. They are not provided with any housing. They are employed by different companies. Calculate the tax to be deducted from their salaries in January 1978:

Kariuki's Salary: Shs. 3,400, or £170.

	Shs.
Tax on £170 = on £100 @ 2/- per £	200
on £ 70 @ 3/- per £	210
on £170 before relief	410
Less: Family Relief	140
Tax Deducted by his employer	270

Wambui's Salary: Shs. 2,200, or £110.

Tax on £110 = on £100 @ 2/- per £	200
on £ 10 @ 3/- per £	30
Tax deducted by her employer	230

If we calculate the total tax deducted from Kariuki's salary in 1978 it will amount to Shs. 3,240 (Shs. 270 x 12). Total tax deducted from Wambui's salary will amount to Shs. 2,760 (Shs. 230 x 12). Thus total tax deducted from the couple will be Shs. 6,000 (Shs. 3,240 + 2,760). But if we calculate tax on their combined salaries it will amount to Shs. 9,120 as follows:

			Shs.
Total Salary:	Kariuki £170 x 12 = £2,040		
	Wambui £110 x 12 = £1,320		
	Tax Chargeable Income	£3,360	
Tax on £3,360:	on £1,200 @ 2/- per £		2,400
	on £1,200 @ 3/- per £		3,600
	on £ 960 @ 5/- per £		4,800
	Tax before relief		10,800
	Less Family Relief		1,680
	Net Tax for 1978		9,120

It will be noticed that net tax on the couple's earnings for 1978, Shs. 9,120, exceeds the tax deducted from their salaries (Shs. 6,000) by Shs. 3,120. At the end of 1978 when Mr Kariuki sends his tax return to Income Tax Department he will be asked to pay this additional sum of Shs. 3,120.

INCOME FROM MORE THAN ONE SOURCE

If a person has more than one source of income, and if tax is deducted at only one or some but not all of the sources, he may find that at the end of year he is asked to pay a large amount of tax. The main reason for it is that when different employers deduct tax they do so at the minimum rates, whereas when all amounts earned are totalled, the tax rate bracket rises, thereby making the person liable to a higher tax.

Example 18:

Mr Katembo earned the following amounts in 1978:

Salary, £2,400.
House Rent, £300.
Rent Received from a tenant, £600.

Mrs Katembo was also employed in 1978 and earned a salary of £1,800.

Calculate the amount that Mr Katembo will have to pay to

the Income Tax Department at the end of the year in addition
to the tax deducted at source by his and his wife's employers.

Step 1: Calculate tax deducted by Mr Katembo's employer by
way of P.A.Y.E.

		Shs.
On £1,200 @ 2/- per £		2,400
£1,200 @ 3/- per £		3,600
£ 300 @ 5/- per £		1,500
Gross Tax on £2,700 before relief		7,500
Less Family Relief		1,680
Tax Deducted by Katembo's employer		5,820

Note: Mr Katembo's chargeable pay will amount to
£2,700 (£2,400 plus house rent received £300).

Step 2: Calculate tax deducted by Mrs Katembo's employer by
way of P.A.Y.E.

	Shs.
On £1,200 @ 2/- per £	2,400
£ 600 @ 3/- per £	1,800
Gross Tax deducted (no relief)	4,200

Step 3: Now calculate total tax liability for the couple including
the rent they have received from their tenant on which
for obvious reasons no tax was deducted at source.

	£
Mr Katembo's salary	2,400
Mr Katembo's House Allowance	300
Mrs Katembo's salary	1,800
Rent from tenant	600
Total Earnings (Chargeable pay)	5,100

	Shs.
Tax on £1,200 @ 2/- per £	2,400
on £1,200 @ 3/- per £	3,600
on £1,200 @ 5/- per £	6,000
on £1,200 @ 7/- per £	8,400
on £ 300 @ 9/- per £	2,700
Tax on £5,100 before relief	23,100
Less Family Relief	1,680
Net Tax	21,420

Step 4: Amount due at the end of 1978 from Mr Katembo in
addition to tax deducted at source will be calculated
as follows:

	Shs.	Shs.
Net Tax		21,420
Less Deducted from Mr Katembo	5,820	
Deducted from Mrs Katembo	4,200	10,020
		11,400

Students are advised to obtain and study a copy of Employers
Guide to P.A.Y.E. issued by Income Tax Department.

QUESTIONS

1. Give at least two reasons to prove that the system of deducting
   income tax at source by way of P.A.Y.E. is of advantage to
   both the taxpayer and the government.
2. What is a Tax Deduction Card? Is it necessary to use the tax
   deduction cards issued by the Income Tax Department? What
   alternatives, if any, are available?
3. Draw up and properly label a Tax Deduction Card for a large
   company that wishes to use its own cards instead of the ones
   issued by the Income Tax Department.
4. Rashid and Yusuf are employed by a trading company. Rashid
   is married and has two children, whereas Yusuf is single with
   no children. Rashid has been provided with a house by the
   company for which he pays a monthly rent of Shs. 300. Yusuf
   is paid an allowance in lieu of housing at the rate of Shs. 750
   per month. Record the following in their Tax Deduction Cards:

Month (Earnings)	Rashid	Yusuf
1978	Shs.	Shs.
January	2,000	1,200
February	900	800
March	1,250	1,160
April	1,780	2,200
May	2,140	600

5. Onyango and Otieno are employed persons. Onyango is married
   but does not have any child, whereas Otieno is single but maintains two children under the age of 18. Both have been given
   houses by their employer and pay a monthly rent of Shs. 100
   each. From the following list of their basic salary in the first
   five months of 1978, prepare their tax deduction cards.

	Onyango Shs.	Otieno Shs.
January	1,200	500
February	1,200	600
March	1,380	700
April	1,800	1,100
May	1,390	1,220

6. Ngugi is employed as a supervisor by a manufacturing company at a monthly salary of Shs. 4,200. He is provided with a furnished house for which he pays Shs. 400 each month to his employer. This amount includes Shs. 50 for furniture and Shs. 40 for water and conservancy. He is married and has two children, both under the age of 18. In July 1978 his pay was increased to Shs. 4,500 per month. In September 1978 he was paid a bonus of Shs. 15,000. Prepare his Tax Deduction Card for the whole of 1978, showing separately your calculation of income tax on bonus payment.

7. Basic facts as for Problem 6. Now assume that Mr Ngugi was paid the bonus in March 1978 at which time it was not known that his pay will be increased in July. Calculate:
   - (a) the amount of income tax on bonus deductible in March,
   - (b) the amount of tax that he will have to pay over and above the amount deducted at source by way of P.A.Y.E., at the end of the year when he is sent his assessment.

8. Kihara and his wife, Wambui, work for different employers. The following is the list of their earnings from employment in 1978:

	Kihara Shs.	Wambui Shs.
Basic Pay	36,000	24,000
Housing Allowance	Nil	4,800
House Rent deducted by Employer	3,600	Nil
Bonus	Nil	5,000

Calculate:
   - (a) the amount of income tax deducted at source by Kihara's employers.
   - (b) the amount of income tax deducted at source by Wambui's employers.
   - (c) the net income tax liability of the couple for 1978, assuming that Kihara pays an annual premium of Shs. 3,000 on own life policy and of Shs. 2,500 on his wife's life policy.

9. Swaleh and his wife, Amina, work for different employers. They provide you with the following information relating to 1978:

	Swaleh Shs.	Amina Shs.
Basic Pay	12,600	18,000
Pension	30,000	30,000
Income from Rent	6,000	Nil

The following additional information is also available:
  (a) Swaleh is provided with furnished housing by his employer for which he pays a monthly rent of Shs. 200 inclusive of Shs. 30 for furniture and Shs. 20 for water.
  (b) They pay a total of Shs. 6,000 per year on their life insurance policies.

Calculate:

  (a) the amount of income tax deducted at source by Swaleh's employer,
  (b) the amount of income tax deducted at source by Amina's employer, and
  (c) the net income tax liability of the couple for 1978.

Chapter Six

BUSINESS PROFITS

ACCOUNTING PERIOD

If a person makes up the accounts of his business for a period of 12 months ending on any day other than 31st December, then to assess tax, the income of his accounting period shall be deemed to be his taxable income for the year in which his accounting year ends, unless the Commissioner of Income Tax considers an adjustment appropriate.

DETERMINING BUSINESS PROFIT

In this chapter we will discuss the profits made by un-incorporated forms of business ownership, i.e. sole proprietors and partnerships. It should be noted that profit from a business constitutes only one source of income for an individual. Thus a person may be employed as well as be owner of a business, or businesses. In his annual tax return he must list his emoluments from employment as one source of income and profit from his business as another. However, if a person is devoting the whole of his time to a business, the profit from that business would be his only income.

Proper accounts are essential if business profits are to be correctly calculated for tax purposes. The absence of proper accounts may result in an overcharge to tax, or in an undercharge which may later have serious consequences. Many traders use the services of qualified practising accountants who prepare their accounts and negotiate with the income tax department the most favourable assessment permitted by law.

Profits as shown by accounts are usually not the same as admissible for tax assessment. There are certain items of expenditure that may reasonably be charged to Profit and Loss (or revenue) Account by a trader that are not allowable for tax purposes. Similarly there are certain receipts that may be credited to the Profit and Loss Account by a trader which are not considered an income by the tax department. It is therefore necessary that the profit shown by the accounts be adjusted to exclude un-allowable items in order to arrive at profit that may be used as a basis for computation of income tax.

The general principle is that for the purpose of arriving at taxable profit only revenue (as distinct from capital) incomes and expenditure should be accounted for.

EXPENSES ALLOWED TO BE DEDUCTED FROM PROFITS

Any sums expended wholly and exclusively for the purpose of the business may usually be deducted from gross profit unless the expenditure is of a capital nature. Among the sums allowable are the following:

1. Bad Debts
   - (a) Only specific debts written off are permitted. A general provision for bad debts calculated as a percentage of debtors is not allowed.
   - (b) Only those bad debts are allowed which result from debts extended for the purpose of business. Thus failure to recover a loan given to a relative will not be considered a bad debt for tax purposes.
2. Capital allowances as specified in the second schedule of the Income Tax Act. These will be discussed briefly later in this chapter and in detail in the next chapter.
3. Any capital expenditure incurred by the owner or occupier of farm land for the prevention of soil erosion.
4. Legal expenses, if of revenue nature, e.g.
   - (a) Legal costs and stamp duties in connection with acquisition of lease for not more than 99 years.
   - (b) Collecting book debts.
   - (c) Settling disputes with customers.
   - (d) Defending existing trade rights.
   - (e) Preparing service agreements, etc.
5. In case of the owner of the premises sums expended for structural alterations to the premises where such expense is necessary to maintain the existing rent income.
6. Any expenditure incurred in connection with any business before the date of commencement of such business where such expenditure would have been deductible if incurred after the commencement of the business.
7. In case of utensils, etc. the Commissioner of Income Tax may allow the amount for wear and tear which he considers just and reasonable.
8. Entrance fees and subscriptions paid to trade association.
9. Cost or value attributable to standing timber sold, or to the rights to fell timber sold by way of business.

10. Cost of rights to fell standing timber attributable to timber sold.
11. Dividends paid or credited to resident persons by a building society.
12. Capital expenditure by owner or tenant of agricultural land on clearing the land, or on clearing and planting on it permanent or semi-permanent crops.
13. Scientific Research Expenditure

    (a) Capital as well and revenue expenditure incurred on scientific research is allowed.
    (b) Any sums paid to any scientific research organisation, approved by the Commissioner of Income Tax, that undertakes research in a field related to the business.
    (c) Any sums paid to any university, college, research institution or similar body that carries out research related to the field of business.

    Thus if a business engaged in textile business pays a sum to an organisation or institution that carries out research in textiles it would be allowed as a business expense; but if the business pays a sum to, say, animal husbandry research institution it would not be allowable.

14. Any expenditure incurred on mining of specified minerals.
15. National provident fund or other retirement benefits schemes established for employees by the provision of any written law. Thus an employer's contribution to the National Social Security Fund in respect of his employees is considered his (employer's) business expense allowable for tax purposes.
16. Any expenditure on advertising in connection with the business to the extent the Commissioner of Income Tax considers just and reasonable. Expenditure incurred on installation of permanent signs is considered a capital expenditure and is not allowable for the purpose of calculating the taxable profit for a particular year.
17. In case of an individual who carries on either alone or in partnership one of the recognised professions, a housing deduction equal to 15% of gains or profits from his profession or Shs. 14,000 per annum, whichever is less, is allowable.
18. Interest paid on money borrowed and used in the production of income from the business.
19. Amount of interest paid in respect of such year of income upon amount not exceeding Shs. 200,000 borrowed from a bank, or a financial institution specified in the fourth schedule of the Income Tax Act, and applied for the purposes of a

house or improvements of it.

Conditions: (a) Must be a residential building.
     (b) One person must not claim this allowance for more than one residential building.

DEDUCTIONS NOT ALLOWED

The following is a summary of those items of expenditure which may appear in the financial accounts of a business but which are not allowed for tax purposes. These items should therefore be added to profits, or deducted from losses, disclosed by the accounts to arrive at the profit or loss for tax purposes.

1. Any expenditure or loss which is not wholly and exclusively incurred in the production of income from business.
2. Any capital expenditure.
3. Any expenditure incurred by any person on the maintenance of himself, his family, or for any other personal or domestic purpose.
4. Any expenditure or loss which is recoverable under any insurance.
5. Any income tax, or tax of a similar nature paid on income.
6. Any premium paid under any annuity contract.
7. Business losses will not be allowed as a deduction if the Commissioner of Income Tax regards the business as not being carried on mainly with a view to the realisation of profits.
   Any business where more than 25% of revenue expenditure relates to goods or benefits of personal or domestic nature enjoyed by any person having a beneficial interest in the business is considered as carried on *not* with a view to making profits.
8. Appropriation of profits, for example any sums transferred to reserves, interest on partners' capitals or loans, salaries paid to sole proprietor or partners, etc.
9. Any sums expended on improvements or additions to premises, plant, machinery, etc.
10. Preliminary expenses, cost of raising loans, etc.
11. Legal expenses, if:

    (a) of a capital nature, for example in respect of preparing a deed of partnership.
    (b) incurred in defending a breach of law. Fines and penalties for breach of law are also disallowed as these are losses not connected with or arising out of trade or business activities.

12. Travelling expenses of the proprietor, or partners, of a business between residence and business premises.
13. Donations.
14. Provisions for depreciation. (See paragraph on Capital Allowances below.)

CAPITAL ALLOWANCES

These are discussed in detail in the next chapter. Briefly these allowances are of three types as follows:

(a) *Investment Allowance*

This allowance, equal to 20% of capital expenditure, is allowed only in the first year of expenditure. It is intended to be an incentive to businessmen to expand their businesses.

(b) *Wear and Tear Allowance*

This may be treated as an equivalent of depreciation. It differs from asset to asset. Exact rates are given in the Second Schedule of the Income Tax Act. Briefly these are:

(i) 2½% on cost of industrial buildings.
(ii) 37½% on written down value of machinery items Class I. These include tractors, heavy earth-moving equipment and such other heavy self-propelling machines.
(iii) 25% on written down value of machines Class II. These include motor vehicles and aircraft.
(iv) 12½% on written down value of other machines, including ships, furniture, office equipment, etc.

(c) *Balancing Allowance or Charge*

This arises in the event of disposal of fixed assets. See next chapter for details.

RECEIPTS NOT CONSIDERED INCOME FOR TAX PURPOSES

The following receipts are not considered as incomes for the purpose of computing taxable profits:

(a) Proceeds of sale of a fixed asset. However, profit arising on disposal of land, buildings and investment shares is liable to capital gains tax. Profit on sale of other fixed assets, e.g. furniture, motor vehicles, etc., gives rise to a balancing charge. See next chapter for details of balancing charge. As a general rule, profit or loss (or even the proceeds of sale) arising on sale of a fixed asset is to be excluded from Profit and Loss Account when computing taxable profit.

(b) Income from overseas investments.
(c) Reduction in general provisions for bad debts.
(d) In the case of partnership, any amount transferred from a Reserve to Profit and Loss (or Appropriation) Account.
(e) Additional capital introduced by the owner or partners.
(f) Recovery of a bad debt which when written off was not allowed as a deduction for tax purposes. For example, if a businessman loans a sum of money for reasons other than trading activities and the loan proves irrecoverable, it cannot be charged to Profit and Loss Account for tax computation purposes. If subsequently this loan is recovered, it will not be treated as an income of the business.
(g) Incomes exempted from income tax under First Schedule of the Income Tax, e.g. interest received on tax reserve certificates.

METHOD OF ADJUSTING PROFIT

The usual method adopted to adjust the accounts of a business for income tax purposes is as follows:

1. Take the net profit as shown by the Profit and Loss (or Revenue) Account.
2. Add back any items debited in the account which are not allowed for tax purposes.
3. Deduct
   (i)   any items credited in the accounts which may properly be eliminated, e.g. gain of a capital nature.
   (ii) any items which not charged in the account, may be deducted for income tax purposes.

Where the Profit and Loss Account shows a net loss the procedure shown above may be reversed.

Example 19:

The following is the Profit and Loss Account of K. Mutiso who has carried on business for many years as a retail hardware merchant.

PROFIT AND LOSS ACCOUNT
for the year ended 31st December 1977

	£		£
Wages and Salaries	2,500	Gross Profit	5,748
Rent and Rates	402	Discounts Received	52
Repairs to Premises	253		

	£		£
Telephone	90	Profit on sale of motor	
Salary to Mrs Mutiso	260	vehicle	50
Advertising	40		
Motor car expenses	376		
Legal charges	11		
Net Profit	1,918		
	5,850		5,850

Notes:

(a) Advertising expenses include the following:

Advertising in local newspapers, £13.
Advertising in a church magazine, £4.
Cost of installing an electric neon sign, £23.

(b) Mutiso resides on the premises and one-third of rent and rates relate to private use.

(c) Legal charges are for renewal of a lease for 25 years.

(d) Motor car expenses include £11 for a fine imposed on Mutiso for exceeding the speed limit while delivering goods to a customer. One-fifth of the car expenses are attributable to personal use.

(e) The book value of furniture used in business was £800 on 1st January 1977. Mutiso has not provided for any depreciation on furniture as he considers none is necessary.

Computation of Mutiso's Adjusted Net Profit for 1977

	£	£
Net Profit per Profit & Loss Account		1,918
Add *Expenses Not Allowed*	£	
Fine for exceeding speed limit	11	
Private use of motor car 1/5th of £365 (£376 - 11)	73	
Advertising—Installing electric sign	23	
Mrs Mutiso's salary	260	
Private rent and rates 1/3rd of £402	134	501
		2,419
Less *Income Not Taxable*		
Profit on sale of motor vehicle		50
Adjusted Profit		2,369

£

	£
Less Wear and Tear Allowance on furniture @ 12½% on £800	100
Net Taxable Profit	2,269

Notes: (1) Salary paid to Mrs Mutiso is considered an· appropriation of profit, not a business expense.

(2) For the purpose of calculating amount of motor car expenses attributable to personal use, the sum of £11 (fine for speeding) must be deducted from total motor car expenses.

(3) Fine for over-speeding is not allowed as a business expense even if the offence was committed when Mr Mutiso was on business duty.

Example 20:

The following is the Profit and Loss Account of A. Musa who has carried on retail business since 1966. Compute the adjusted profit for income tax purposes, and state the net amount after capital allowance adjustments.

A. MUSA
PROFIT AND LOSS ACCOUNT FOR THE YEAR 1977

	£		£
Salaries: Staff	2,400	Gross Profit	8,740
Self	1,300	Dividends re-	
Wife	400	ceived (net)	170
National Social Security		Reduction in General	
Fund Contributions	130	Provision for Bad	
Rent and Rates	540	Debts	54
Light and Heat	165		
Repairs	90		
Motor car expenses	520		
Interest on loan (for purchase of equipment)	45		
Accountant's Fees	60		
Sundry Expenses	98		
Depreciation: Equipment	115		
Motor Car	240		
Balance c/d (Net Profit)	2,861		
	8,964		8,964

	£		£
Income Tax	856	Balance b/f	
Goodwill written off	300	(Net Profit)	2,861
Balance transferred to capital account	1,705		
	2,861		2,861

Notes: (a) On 1st January 1977 A. Musa's fixed assets had the following written down values:

> Equipment £560
> Motor Car £480

On 30th August 1977 A. Musa bought new equipment for £200 and one month later a new motor car for £1,200.

(b) No entry has been made in the books for goods, valued at £250, taken by A. Musa for personal consumption.

(c) A. Musa lives over the shop premises. One-third of rent and rates, and light and heat is for his domestic use.

(d) One-quarter of motor car expenses are attributable to private use.

(e) Repair expenses comprise of the following items:

> Decorating shop, £38
> Decorating bedrooms, £40
> Repairing shop refrigerator, £12.

(f) Sundry expenses are analysed as follows:

> Printing and paper, £57
> Fees for a shop assistant's attendance on a trade course at Kenya Polytechnic, £30
> Subscription to local chamber of commerce, £5
> Fine for employing an under-aged employee, £6.

First we should compute the Wear & Tear Allowance (Capital Allowance) for Equipment and Motor Vehicles.

		£
Equipment:	Written-down value on 1.1.1977	560
	Add: new purchases	200
	Book-value on 31.12.1977	760

Capital Allowance @ 12½% of £760 = £95

		£
Motor Car:	Written-down value on 1.1.1977	480
	Add: new purchase	1,200
	Book-value on 31.12.1977	1,680

Capital Allowance @ 25% of £1,680 = £420.

Note: A full year's allowance is given for machines even if they are used for only one day in the year.

Computation of A. Musa's Adjusted Net Profit for 1977

		£
Profit per Profit and Loss Account		2,861
Add *Expenses Not Allowed*	£	
Depreciation on Equipment	115	
Depreciation on Motor Cars	240	
Fine for employing an under-aged person	6	
Private Motor Car Expenses (¼ of £520)	130	
Cost of Decorating Bedrooms	40	
Private occupation of Premises		
1/3rd of £540 (Rent & Rates)	180	
1/3rd of £165 (Light & Heat)	55	
Salaries (Self £1,300 + Wife £400)	1,700	2,466
		5,327
Less: *Incomes not taxable*		
Dividends Received (net)	170	
Reduction in General Provision for Bad Debts	54	224
		5,103
Add: Goods for own use		250
Adjusted Profit		5,353
Less: Capital Allowances		
Wear & Tear Allowance on Equipment	95	
Wear & Tear Allowance on Motor Cars	420	515
Net Taxable Profit		4,838

Notes: (a) Dividends received (net) are not considered a business income as it does not relate to the trading activities. However Mr Musa must show this receipt as an income when preparing his personal tax return.

(b) Reduction in general provisions for bad debts is also not considered a business income for tax purposes because when these provisions were created (in previous years) they were not considered a business expense.

TREATMENT OF BUSINESS LOSSES

If, after adjusting business profits (or loss), for tax purpose the figure arrived at shows a loss, the loss may be off set against profits of future years.

Example 21:

Mr Karanja incurred a net loss, after adjustments, for 1976 of £3,200. In 1977 he made a net profit, after adjustments of £5,600. He has no other source of income. What will be his chargeable income of 1977.

		£
Chargeable Income of 1977:	Net Profit	5,600
	Less Loss of 1976	3,200
		2,400

Thus Mr Karanja will pay no income tax in 1976 and for 1977 his tax will be computed as if his income were only £2,400.

INCOME AND EXPENDITURE AFTER THE CESSATION OF BUSINESS

If any sum is received by any person after the cessation of his business which would have been included in the gains or profits of the business had it been received before its cessation, such sum is treated as the income of the person for the year in which it is received.

If any sum is paid by any person after the cessation of his business which would have been allowed as a deduction for the purpose of determining his income had it been paid before the cessation of business, such payment would be allowed as a deduction for the year in which it is made. If such payment cannot be offset in that year then it can be deducted in ascertaining his total income for the year of income in which his business ceased.

PARTNERSHIP PROFITS

In case of partnership the adjusted profit is computed in the same manner as of a sole proprietor. Any sums paid to partners as salary, interest on capital, etc. that may have been charged to Profit and Loss Account should be added back to Net Profit as these are not considered an expense but an appropriation of profit for tax purposes.

The adjusted profit is divided between partners after allowing for interest on capital, salary, etc. as stipulated in their partnership deed. Each partner's tax liability is computed separately. His total income from partnership is taken to be the total of all sums credited to his capital (or current) account from Profit and Loss Appropriation Account (viz. interest on capitals, salary, commission, etc.)

A Partnership Return Form must be completed each year by the precedent partner. If the precedent partner is not an active partner, the return form must be completed by the precedent resident partner. This form specifies the total income of the partnership and also the shares of the individual partners. In addition each partner must also complete his personal return form showing his income from all sources including his share of profits from partnership.

Example 22:

Ahmad, Bakar and Cheka are partners sharing profits and losses equally after allowing interest on capitals as follows:

> Ahmad, £300
> Bakar, £200
> Cheka, £150

and after allowing partnership salaries of £500 and £300 to Ahmad and Cheka respectively. The adjusted profits for the year 1978 before allowing interest on capitals and salaries was £5,950.

Apportionment of Profits Between Ahmad, Bakar and Cheka

		£	£
Adjusted Profit			5,950
Less: Interest on capitals:	Ahmad	300	
	Bakar	200	
	Cheka	150	
Partnership salaries:	Ahmad	500	
	Cheka	300	
			1,450
Balance divisible equally			4,500

	Total	Ahmad	Bakar	Cheka
	£	£	£	£
Interest on Capitals	650	300	200	150
Salaries	800	500	— —	300
Share of Profit	4,500	1,500	1,500	1,500
	5,950	2,300	1,700	1,950

Example 23:

Basic facts as for Example 22. Assuming that Bakar is a full-time employee of Moto Fireworks Ltd. and earns an annual salary of £2,400 from his employment, calculate his (a) Chargeable Income for 1978 and (b) tax liability for the same year. You are also told that Bakar is married and does not receive any house allowance from his employers as he resides in his personal house.

Bakar's Earnings for 1978

	£
Income from employment	2,400
Partnership Profits: Interest on Capital	200
Share of Profit	1,500
Chargeable Income	4,100

Computation of Tax Liability

	Shs.
On first £1,200 @ 2/= per £	2,400
On next £1,200 @ 3/= per £	3,600
On next £1,200 @ 5/= per £	6,000
On next £500 @ 7/= per £	3,500
On £4,100	15,500
Less: Family Relief	1,680
Tax Liability for 1978	13,820

If the adjusted profit of a partnership is less than the amount required to meet the salaries of partners and interest on capitals, the apportionment should be made in accordance with the terms of their partnership agreement. Where in such circumstances a partner's adjusted share is a *'loss'*, this loss can be off-set against any other income that he may have in that year, or can be carried forward and off-set against any income in future years without any time limit.

Example 24:

Daudi, Elimu and Fundi are in partnership sharing profits and losses in the ratio one-half, one-fifth and three-tenths respectively. Daudi is entitled to an annual salary of £400. Interest on capitals is allowed as follows:

Daudi £80
Elimu £60
Fundi £20

The adjusted profit for the year 1978 before providing for partner's salary and interest on capitals amounted to £450.

Computation of Divisible Profits or Losses

	£	£
Adjusted Profit		450
Less: Daudi's salary	400	
Interest on Capitals: Daudi	80	
Elimu	60	
Fundi	20	
		560
Loss divisible between partners		110

Apportionment of Loss Between Partners

	Total	Daudi	Elimu	Fundi
	£	£	£	£
Salary	400	400	––	––
Interest on Capital	160	80	60	20
	560	480	60	20
Less Share of Loss	110	55	22	33
	450	425	38	(13)
	Profit	Profit	Profit	Loss

Daudi and Elimu are liable for tax in 1978. If Fundi has any other source of income in 1978 he can deduct his loss of £13 from any such income, or he can carry forward this amount to next year and off-set it against profits of future years if he has no source of income other than profits from partnership.

Example 25:

Chengo and Kisaka are in partnership sharing profits and losses equally after charging interest on capitals, Chengo £200 and Kisaka £100, and after allowing for an annual salary of £600 to Kisaka.

Chengo is married with three children. He pays an annual premium of £200 on his own life insurance policy and of £140 on a policy on his wife's life. Kisaka is single but has a child under 18 years of age whom he maintains. He also pays an annual insurance premium of £100 on his personal life insurance policy.

Following is their Profit and Loss Account for the year ended

31st December 1978:

Profit and Loss and Appropriation Account for 1978

	£		£
Salaries: Staff	5,786	Gross Profit	13,875
Kisaka	600	Reduction in speci-	
Rent and Rates	675	fic bad debts pro-	
Electricity	320	vision	54
Repairs	432		
Subscriptions to local			
Trade Association	80		
Donation to charities	110		
Legal Costs:			
Renewal of 18 years lease 10			
Alteration to partnership			
Agreement 15	25		
Depreciation on fixed assets	860		
Bad Debts written off	130		
Interest on Capitals:			
Chengo	200		
Kisaka	100		
Total Expenses	10,077		
Net Profit c/f	3,852		
	13,929		13,929
Share of Profit: Chengo	1,926	Net Profit b/f	3,852
Kisaka	1,926		
	3,852		3,852

Notes:

(a) Repairs include £200 for extension of office building.
(b) Bad Debts written off include a sum of £50 that was loaned in cash to a customer who was in financial troubles.
(c) Goods taken from the business for own consumption by partners not included in the books were estimated as follows:

        Chengo £200
        Kisaka £241

(d) Assume that the partners are not entitled to any capital allowance for wear and tear of their fixed assets.

Compute (a) Adjusted Profit of Partnership.
          (b) Income of each partner from the partnership.
          (c) Assuming that partners have no source of income

other than the partnership earnings, compute their tax liability.

Computation of Adjusted Profit of Chengo and Kisaka for the Year 1978

	£	£
Profit as per Profit and Loss Account		3,852
Add: *Expenses not allowed for Tax Purposes*		

	£	£
Interest on Capital	300	
Bad Debts written off	50	
Depreciation on fixed assets	860	
Legal costs for alteration to partnership deed	15	
Donations to charities	110	
Repairs — extensions of building	200	
Kasaka's salary	600	
Drawings in form of goods: Kasaka	241	
Chengo	200	2,576
Adjusted Profit		6,428

Apportionment of Profit Between Partners

	Total £	Chengo £	Kisaka £
Interest on capitals	300	200	100
Salary	600	—	600
Share of Profit (½ of balance each)	5,528	2,764	2,764
	6,428	2,964	3,464

Tax Liability of Chengo

Business Profits, £2,964 (as per the above statement)

	Shs.
Tax on first £1,200 @ 2/= per £	2,400
on next £1,200 @ 3/= per £	3,600
on next £564 @ 5/= per £	2,820
Total tax on £2,964	8,820

	Shs.	
Less: Family Relief	1,680	
Insurance Relief (maximum)	480	2,160
Tax Liability for 1978		6,660

Tax Liability of Kisaka

Business Profits, £3,464 (as per the statement above)

		Shs.
Tax on first £1,200 @ 2/= per £		2,400
on next £1,200 @ 3/= per £		3,600
on next £864 @ 5/= per £		4,320
Tax on £3,464		10,320
Less: Special Single Relief	720	
Insurance Relief @ 2/= per £ on £100	200	
		920
Tax Liability for 1978		9,400

Notes:

(a) No adjustment is necessary in respect of reduction in provisions for specific bad debts as these were allowable when originally created.

(b) Bad Debt of £50 which was loaned in cash to a customer is not allowable as such loaning of money is not a usual trade activity.

(c) Legal costs for alteration to partnership deed are treated as preliminary expenses, hence a capital expenditure which is not allowable for tax purposes.

(d) If the tax is paid out of partnership bank account, the amounts should be debited to Drawings Accounts of partners.

QUESTIONS

1. List the expenses that are not allowable deductions for the purpose of computing business profits.
2. List the expenses that are allowable deductions for the purpose of computing business profits.
3. List the items that may reasonably be credited to the Profit and Loss Account of a business but that are not considered an income for income tax purposes.
4. List the items that may reasonably be debited to Profit and Loss Appropriation Account of a partnership business but that are not considered an expense for income tax purposes.
5. Briefly outline the powers of the Commissioner of Income Tax regarding inspection of books of accounts.
6. Is it essential that financial year of every individual businessman must coincide with the calendar year? What is treated to be a year of income if the financial year of a business-

man ends on a date other than 31st December each year?

7. Describe the method of adjusting profit as shown by Profit and Loss Account to arrive at profit chargeable to income tax.

8. How are business losses treated?

9. Who fills in a partnership return of income form?

10. Is the business of an individual treated as an entity separate from him? What is the position regarding businesses run by partners?

11. What documents must be attached with the return of income filed by a businessman? Is the situation any different if the accounts of a businessman are maintained by a practising accountant?

12. Who is a precedent resident partner?

13. James Karibi is a businessman. He is married and has two sons, both over the age of 18 but at school. He made a net profit of £4,280 in 1978 after charging the following items to his Profit and Loss Account:

		£
Salaries: Self		2,400
Staff		2,140
General Provisions for bad debts		110
Bad Debts written off		235
Profit on sale of a motor vehicle		200
Advertising		320
Legal charges		45
Improvements to business premises		1,200
Insurance: Own life policy		300
Wife's insurance policy		200
Business premises		164
Depreciation on fixed assets		1,170

Notes:

(a) Advertising expenses include a payment of £200 made for instalation of a permanent neon sign.

(b) Legal charges are composed of:

Parking fines while on official work	£10
Preparation of lease agreement for 25 years	15
Recovery of bad debts (lawyers' fees)	20

(c) Mr Karibi is not entitled to any capital deduction on fixed assets.

(d) Bad debts written off include an amount of £50 loaned in cash to a customer who was in financial difficulties.

(e) Mrs Karibi is employed as a secretary in a company and earns an annual salary of £900 against which a

PAYE of Shs. 1,800 has been deducted by her employer. Mr Karibi is in receipt of pension amounting to £600 per annum.

Calculate the tax liability of Mr James Karibi.

14. Paul Kahika is married with three children. He runs a business of a wholesaler. In 1978 his Profit and Loss Account revealed a net profit of £21,640 after charging/including the following items:

	£
Salary: Mrs Kahika	2,400
Mr Kahika	3,600
Staff	9,640
Motor Running Expenses (excluding depreciation)	1,080
Telephone & Electricity	300
Rent and Rates	3,000
Legal charges	220
Discounts Received	480
Income from sub-let	1,200
Income from overseas investments	1,800
Reduction in general provisions for bad debts	220
Depreciation on fixed assets	4,900
General Expenses	3,240
Insurance: Business premises	480
Life insurance — Mr Kahika	300
Interest on tax reserve certificates	80
Drawings in addition to salaries	1,870

Notes:

(a) Mr Kahika is not entitled to any capital deductions on fixed assets.

(b) Legal charges include £50 for parking fines while on official business, and a fine of £100 for employing a non-citizen in the business. The balance of legal charges is for preparing lease for business premises for 10 years.

(c) A part of the business premises are occupied by Mr Kahika as residence. A quarter of the expenses relating to the premises, telephone and electricity, are a attributable to personal use.

(d) Personal and private use of motor car is assessed at one-third of total use.

(e) General expenses include the cost of a sofa set, £200, bought as a present by Mr Kahika to his eldest son who is married and lives separately.

(f) Mr Kahika has no other source of income.

Compute Mr Kahika's income tax liability for 1978.

15. Duncan Mubiru and Peter Mukasa are running a business in partnership. Mr Mubiru is married and has two children, both at school. Peter Mukasa is not married but maintains a child under the age of 18. Their Profit and Loss and Appropriation Account for 1978 is as follows:

Profit and Loss and Appropriation Account

	£		£
Salaries: Staff	6,850	Gross Profit	16,700
Mubiru	2,400	Interest on Tax	
Rent and Rates	3,840	Reserve Certifi-	
Legal Expenses	380	cates	640
Power and Heat	660	Profit on sale of	
Interest on capitals		motor car	500
Mubiru	300	Net Loss: Mubiru	2,000
Mukasa	600	Mukasa	2,000
Repairs & Maintenance	2,800		
Subscriptions to:			
Local Trade Association	30		
Local Chamber of Commer-			
ce	20		
Depreciation on furniture	800		
General Expenses	3,160		
	21,840		21,840

Notes:

(a) Ignore capital allowances, balancing charge, etc.

(b) Legal charges comprise:

Parking and other fines	£ 50
Amendment of partnership deed	150
Preparation of business premises lease	170
Recovering bad debts	10

(c) Repairs and maintenance include the cost of £500 of advertising neon sign.

(d) General Expenses comprise:

Insurance of business premises	£ 400
Cost of new furniture	350
Bad Debts written off	100
Specific Provision for bad debts	80
Petrol & Car maintenance	350
Donation to R.I.A.T.	50
Other Expenses (all allowable)	1,830

(e)   Mubiru is in receipt of pension of £1,200 per annum. He pays insurance premium of £600 on his own and his wife's life insurance.

(f)   Mrs Mubiru earns a salary of £1,800 per annum against which PAYE amounting to Shs. 4,200 has been deducted at source. Mr Mukasa has no other source of income apart from business profits.

Compute income tax liability of Mubiru and Mukasa.

Chapter Seven

CAPITAL ALLOWANCES

DEPRECIATION OF FIXED ASSETS

Among the list of items not allowed as a charge against profits of a business is any amount provided for depreciation. There are so many accepted bases of calculating and providing depreciation on fixed assets for accounting purposes, and the amounts so provided could so easily be varied purely to reduce tax liability, that the Income Tax Department has deemed it proper to disallow this item as an expense. However, in lieu of depreciation an allowance for wear and tear on fixed assets is granted under the Income Tax Act. The second schedule of the Act grants capital allowances in respect of capital expenditure on the following assets:

(a) Industrial buildings
(b) Machinery, including motor vehicles, aircraft, ships, etc.
(c) Mining operations
(d) Agricultural land and buildings.

TYPES OF CAPITAL ALLOWANCES

There are three types of capital allowances granted by the Act:

(a) *Investment Allowance*

This allowance is granted mainly as incentive to invest money in capital projects. It is calculated as a percentage of the capital expenditure and is allowed only once in the year in which capital expenditure is incurred. Unlike a wear and tear allowance, investment allowance is not deducted from the cost of a fixed asset to arrive at its written down value.

(b) *Wear and Tear Allowance*

Also known as *writing down allowance* this allowance is an equivalent of depreciation charge. It is calculated as a percentage on the value of the asset and is allowed to the user of the machine. In case of industrial buildings the wear and tear allowance is calculated as a percentage on the *cost* of the fixed asset whereas in the case of machinery it is calculated as a percentage on the *written down value*. It should be noted that the written down value of an asset as shown in the accounts may not be the same as calculated for tax purposes.

(c) *Balancing Allowance/Charge*

This allowance merits detailed explanation which is given below as a separate heading.

BALANCING ALLOWANCE

This allowance results when a fixed asset against which a capital allowance has been received is disposed of. If the amount realised on disposal is less than the written down value (for tax purposes) of the asset, the difference is granted as a balancing allowance. This allowance can be deducted from adjusted profit of the business to arrive at taxable profit. However if the asset sold is immediately replaced the balancing allowance may be added to the cost of the new asset so that in future years a higher wear and tear allowance may be claimed.

Example 26:

The written down value of a lorry is £1,000 on 1st January 1976. It is sold for £800 on 1st July 1976. Wear and Tear allowance on vehicles is 25% of written down value. Show your treatment of balancing allowance if:

(a) no new lorry is bought.
(b) a new lorry is bought for £2,500.

(a) *If no new lorry is bought*

	£
Written down value of the lorry	1,000
Less amount realised on disposal	800
Balancing allowance	200

The sum of £200 can be deducted from 1976's adjusted profit to arrive at taxable profit for that year.

(b) *If a new lorry is bought*

	£
Cost of new lorry	2,500
Add: Balancing Allowance	200
Value of new lorry for tax purposes	2,700

Wear and tear allowance on the new lorry for 1976:
@ 25% of £2,700 = £675.

No balancing allowance will arise if only a part of an asset is sold. In this case the amount realised on disposal will be deducted from the written down value of the asset and future wear and tear allowance calculated on the basis of the new written down value.

Example 27:

A machine against which a wear and tear allowance of 12½% is granted had a written down value of £5,000 on 1st January 1977. A part of the machine was sold for £2,400 on 1st September 1977. Calculate wear and tear allowance for 1977.

	£
Written down value on 1.1.1977	5,000
Less Amount realised on disposal	2,400
Written down value on 31.12.1977	2,600

Wear and tear allowance @ 12½% of £2,600 = £325.

Note: If only a part of the asset is sold, it is unimportant to pay attention to the written down value of the 'part sold'.

Example 28:

If in the above example a new machine was bought for £4,000 immediately after the disposal of a part of the old machine, how would we calculate wear and tear allowance for 1977?

	£
Written down value of old machine (as above)	2,600
Add cost of new machine	4,000
Written down value of 2 machines	6,600

Wear and tear allowance @ 12½% of £6,600 = £825.

Balancing allowance resulting on cessation of business

Where a balancing allowance arises on cessation of the business, it may be deducted from the profit for that year. But if the profit for the year in which a business ceases is less than the balancing allowance, the excess can be carried back and allowed against the total income of the next preceding year of income. The amount can be carried back to a maximum of 6 years. If any income tax has already been paid on the profit for these years, it may be reclaimed from the income tax department.

Example 29:

H. Simba, an old-established businessman, ceased trading on 31st December 1976. His adjusted profit for 1976 amounted to £4,000. The written down value of his fixed assets proved £12,000 more than the amount realised on their disposal. His taxable profits for the previous six years were as follows:

Year	1970	Profit £10,000
	1971	4,000
	1972	8,000
	1973	6,000
	1974	2,000
	1975	3,000

H. Simba's taxable profits will be adjusted as follows:

		£
1976:	Profit	4,000
	Less Capital (balancing) allowance	12,000
	Unused Capital allowance c/f	8,000
	Taxable Profit	Nil
1975:	Profit	3,000
	Less Capital allowance b/f	8,000
	Unused Capital allowance c/f	5,000
	Taxable Profit	Nil
1974:	Profit	2,000
	Less Capital allowance b/f	5,000
	Unused Capital allowance c/f	3,000
	Taxable Profit	Nil
1973:	Profit	6,000
	Less Capital allowance b/f	3,000
	Taxable Profit	3,000

1972, 1971 and 1970: No adjustment necessary.

BALANCING CHARGE

If the amount realised on disposal of an asset is more than its written down value for tax purposes, the difference is called a 'balancing charge'. It can be treated in two ways. If no new asset is bought to replace the one sold, the balancing charge is treated as a taxable profit for the business for the year in which the asset is sold. If a replacement asset is bought, the balancing charge is deducted from its cost to arrive at its written down value for tax purposes. Thus in future years a reduced wear and tear allowance will be claimed. However, no balancing adjustment would be necessary if only a part of the asset is sold.

Example 30:

A machine for which a wear and tear allowance is granted at 12½% on written down value had a written down value of £1,000 on 1st January 1976. It was sold for £1,200 in September 1976. Show your computation of Balancing Charge if no new machine is bought.

	£
Written down value on 1.1.1976	1,000
Amount Realised on Disposal	1,200
Balancing Charge	200

The sum of £200 would be treated as a taxable income for 1976.

Example 31:

Basic facts as in the above example. If a new machine is bought for £3,000 to replace the old machine, what would be the amount allowable for wear and tear in 1976 for the new machine.

	£
Cost of new machine	3,000
Less Balancing Charge	200
Written down value for tax purposes	2,800

Wear and tear Allowance @ 12½% on £2,800 = 350

If an asset is sold for more than its cost, the Balancing Charge is restricted to the excess of cost over written down value. This is so because a Balancing Charge should not exceed the total amount allowed as a wear and tear allowance on an asset.

Example 32

An asset that was bought for £10,000 had a written down value of £8,000 on 1st January 1977. It was sold for £13,000 on 4th April 1977. Calculate Balancing Charge.

	£
Written down value on 1.1.1977	8,000
Amount Realised on Disposal	13,000
Surplus on disposal	5,000

> Total Wear and Tear Allowance provided on the asset to
> the date of disposal £10,000 - £8,000 = £2,000 is
> Balancing Charge.

Balancing Charge may not be more than £2,000 in this case. But if the asset had been sold for, say, £9,600, Balancing Charge would have been £1,600 (£9,600 - £8,000).

The excess of surplus over Balancing Charge is termed as Capital Gain which is liable to a Capital Gains Tax. Capital Gains Tax is discussed in the last chapter of this book. In this case Capital Gains Tax would be charged on £3,000.

CAPITAL ALLOWANCE FOR INDUSTRIAL BUILDINGS

Capital allowances are not granted in respect of all premises but only in respect of those that come within the definition of an 'industrial building' as laid down in the second schedule of the Income Tax Act. To come within the meaning of industrial building, a building must be in use for the purposes of:

(1) (a) a business carried on in a mill, factory or other similar premises, or

   (b) a transport, dock, bridge, tunnel, inland navigation, water, electricity or hydraulic power undertaking, or

   (c) a business which consists in the manufacture of goods or materials or the subjection of goods or materials to any process, or

   (d) a business which consists in the storage of:

   (i)   raw materials,

   (ii) goods which have been manufactured but not yet delivered to a purchaser,

   (iii) goods imported into any part of the partner states,

   or

   (e) a business which consists in ploughing or cultivating land or doing any other agricultural operation on such land.

(2) a dwelling house constructed for and occupied by the employees of a person carrying on one of the above trades.

(3) a building in use for the welfare of workers employed by any business or undertaking referred to in (1) above.

(4) a building which is in use as a hotel or part of a hotel and which the Minister for Finance and Economic Planning has certified to be an industrial building.

The term 'industrial building' does not include any building in use as a dwelling house, retail shop, showroom, and office.

If part of the building is not an industrial building, allowance will be given on that part only which is an industrial building. However allowance may be given for the whole of the building if the capital expenditure incurred on the part that is not an industrial building is not more than 10% of the total capital expenditure incurred on the whole building.

Expenditure on cost of land or for acquiring any rights there-in is not regarded as part of the cost of construction of the building for the purpose of capital allowances, though the cost of preparing, cutting and levelling the land can be added to the cost of construction. Capital allowances are thus granted for 'building' and not for 'premises' or 'land' on which the building stands.

Rates of Allowances on Industrial Buildings

Investment Allowance 20%
Wear and Tear Allowance:
    Hotels 4%
    Industrial Buildings other than hotels ... 2½%

Allowances given on industrial buildings are calculated on cost, i.e. on straight line basis. If a building is used for only a part of a year the wear and tear allowance is proportionately reduced. Thus if a building is used for only 3 months as an industrial building in a year, and its cost is £20,000, wear and tear allowance would be calculated as follows:

Allowance for the year @ 2½% of £20,000   =   £500
Allowance for three months   = $£500 \times {}^{3}/_{12} = £125$.

Wear and Tear allowance is given for only 25 years in case of hotels and for 40 years in case of other industrial buildings. No allowance is given after these periods even if the building continues to be used as an industrial building.

When an industrial building is sold and is continued to be used as an industrial building by the new owner, the wear and tear allowance is apportioned between the purchaser and seller on time basis.

Example 33:

Mugo, an old established businessman, prepares his accounts annually to 31st December. On 1st May 1976 he incurred capital expenditure amounting to £30,000 on construction of an industrial building. This amount includes £6,000 for cost of land. The building was brought into use and continues to be used as an industrial building. Calculate capital allowances for 1976 and 1977.

		£
1976:	Cost of building including land	30,000
	Less Cost of land	6,000
	Cost of construction	24,000
	Investment Allowance @ 20% of £24,000	4,800
	Wear and Tear Allowance @ 2½% of £24,000 = £600 x $\frac{8}{12}$	400
		5,200
1977:	Wear and Tear Allowance @ 2½% of £24,000	600

Notes:
(a) Cost of land must be deducted from total cost of the building as cost of land is not allowable for capital allowance purposes.
(b) Investment Allowance is not subtracted from the cost of building. So that over a period of 40 years the total capital allowance claimed on an industrial building would amount to 120% of the cost.
(c) In 1976 the building was in use for 8 months only, therefore only 8/12th of annual allowance would be given.
(d) In 1977 the allowance is 2½% of £24,000 and not on the written down value of the building.

WEAR AND TEAR ALLOWANCE ON MACHINERY

Capital allowances in respect of capital expenditure on machinery are available to any person carrying on a trade, profession or vocation, or in employment. In order to qualify for a capital allowance the expenditure must be of a capital nature and on machinery which for the purpose of tax includes such items as motor vehicles and furniture, fittings and fixtures of a permanent or durable nature.

The Second Schedule of the Income Tax Act has classified machines as follows:

Class (i) Tractors, combine harvesters, heavy earth-moving equipment and such other heavy self-propelling machines. Wear and Tear Allowance for this class

is 37½% on written down value per year.
(ii) Other self-propelling vehicles, including aircraft. Wear and Tear Allowance: 25% on written down value per year.
(iii) All other machinery, including ships, furniture and fittings, etc. Wear and Tear Allowance: 12½% on written down value per year.

Wear and Tear Allowance is given on written down value which is calculated as follows:

Written down Value at the beginning of the year

Add: Cost of new machines bought during the year
Less: Amounts realised on disposal of any part of the machines duirng the year.

Any expense incurred to alter the building incidental to the installing of machinery is considered a part of the cost of machine. Total allowance cannot exceed the capital expenditure on machinery. Wear and tear allowance must therefore cease when the capital expenditure has been wholly allowed.

Wear and tear allowance is given only on assets which are in use at the end of the accounting year. A full year's allowance is given in the year in which a machine is bought (even if the machine is used for only one day in that year) while no allowance is given in the year in which the asset is disposed of.

Example 34:

A trader whose trading year ends on 31st December bought a machine for £19,200 and spent £800 to alter his buildings to install the machine on 30th September 1974. In 1975 a part of the machine was sold for £4,500 and replaced by a new machine costing £6,000.

Wear and tear allowance will be computed as follows:

Wear and Tear Schedule

		£
1974:	Cost of Machine	19,200
	Add: Cost of altering buildings	800
		20,000
	Less: Wear and Tear Allowance @ 12½%	2,500
1975:	Written down value b/f	17,500
	Less: Disposal of machinery	4,500
		13,000

	£
Add: Purchase of new machinery ,	6,000
	19,000
Less: Wear and Tear Allowance @ 12½%	2,375
	16,625

WEAR AND TEAR ALLOWANCE ON MOTOR VEHICLES

Wear and tear allowance on motor vehicles is 25% on written down value. There is however a provision in the Income Tax Act that if a motor vehicle is capable of being used as a private vehicle, e.g. a motor car, the allowance will be given for a maximum value of £1,500 per car. This implies that if a motor car is bought for a sum larger than £1,500, for tax computation purposes it will be treated as if it is of a value of £1,500. When such a vehicle is sold and a balancing charge or balancing allowance arises, the proceeds of sale of the car will be reduced in the proportion that £1,500 bears to the original cost.

Example 35:

A businessman who makes his accounts to 31st December each year purchased three motor vehicles, one lorry for £4,000 and two saloon motor cars for £2,000 each, on 30th March 1972. Motor Car A was sold on 30th December 1974 for £1,200 and Motor Car B was sold on 30th November 1975 for £1,000. Compute wear and tear allowance upto the end of 1975.

For the sake of clarity we will calculate wear and tear allowance on lorry separately from the allowance on motor cars.

Lorry		£
1972:	Cost of the vehicle	4,000
	Less Wear and Tear Allowance @ 25%	1,000
1973:	Written down value b/f	3,000
	Less Wear and Tear Allowance @ 25%	750
1974:	Written down value b/f	2,250
	Less Wear and Tear Allowance @ 25%	562
1975:	Written down value b/f	1,688
	Less Wear and Tear Allowance @ 25%	422
	Written down value c/f	1,266

Notes:

A full year's allowance is given in the year in which a vehicle is bought.

(b)   Wear and Tear allowance is calculated on written down value, i.e. on reducing instalment method.

Saloon Motor Cars

		£
1972:	Cost of Cars for tax purposes (maximum £1,500 each)	3,000
	Less Wear and Tear Allowance @ 25%	750
1973:	Written down value b/f	2,250
	Less Wear and Tear Allowance @ 25%	562
1974:	Written down value b/f	1,688
	Less Disposal of Car A (See Note 1 below)	900
		788
	Less Wear and Tear Allowance @ 25%	197
1975:	Written down value b/f	591
	Less Disposal of Car B (See Note 2 below)	750
	Balancing Charge (See Note 3 below)	159

Notes:

(1)   Car A was sold for £1,200. But as its cost (£2,000) is more than £1,500, the amount realised on disposal must be reduced in the same proportion as £1,500 bear to the cost of the car. Calculations as follows:

$$\frac{\text{Maximum Amount Allowed}}{\text{Actual Cost of Vehicle}} \text{ x Sale Price}$$

$$= \frac{1,500}{2,000} \text{ x } 1,200 = £900$$

(2)   Car B was sold for £1,000. This amount is reduced to £750 using the same principle as illustrated in the above case.

$$\frac{\text{Maximum Amount Allowed}}{\text{Actual Cost of Vehicle}} \text{ x Sale Price}$$

$$= \frac{1,500}{2,000} \text{ x } 1,000 = £750$$

(3)   Balancing Charge that arises in 1975 (£159) can be deducted from the written down value of the motor lorry, or if the business wishes to keep separate accounts for lorry and motor cars, the sum of £159 can be treated as an income for the year 1975. In the latter case it would

be taxed.

Example 36:

Basic facts as for the foregoing example. Now assume that motor car B was sold for £500 and re-compute the balancing charge or allowance arising out of its disposal.

	£
Written down value on 1.1.1975 (as in above example)	591
Less Disposal of Car B:	
$\dfrac{1,500}{2,000} \times 500 = £375$	375
Balancing Allowance	216

Note:

If it is assumed that the business keeps one account for all its vehicles, the balancing allowance can be added to the written down value of the motor lorry. But if the business wishes to treat lorry and motor vehicles as two separate items (and if the Tax Department agrees to such a proposition), the balancing allowance may be treated as an expense for 1975.

Private Use of Motor Vehicles

If a motor vehicle is used for private as well as business purposes, wear and tear allowance is restricted to the proportion that business use bears to total use.

Example 37:

A trader bought a motor car for £1,200 in 1974. It was agreed with the Tax Department that one-quarter of the use of the car was for private purpose. The vehicle was sold for £599 in 1976.

Computation of Wear and Tear Allowance:		£
1974:	Cost of the Vehicle	1,200
	Less Wear and Tear Allowance @ 25%	300
1975:	Written down Value b/f	900
	Less Wear and Tear Allowance @ 25%	225
1976:	Written down Value b/f	675
	Less Amount realised on disposal	599
	Balancing allowance	76

The above are allowances for the car, but as the car is not fully

used for business purposes, the wear and tear allowance as would
be allowable would be calculated as follows:

1974:   ¾ of £300 = £225
1975:   ¾ of £225 = £169
1976:   Balancing Allowance = ¾ of £76 = £57.

It should be noted that calculation should be made on the total
written down value of the car, deductions should be made in full
to arrive at the written down value, but only the correct proportion should be deducted from the income (or profit) for the
year for tax purposes.

CAPITAL ALLOWANCE IN RESPECT OF AGRICULTURAL LAND

Capital deductions are granted only if the land is used wholly
or mainly for the purposes of a trade of husbandry. Only that
capital expenditure qualifies for an allowance that has been incurred for this purpose. Thus if on an agricultural land a person
builds a hotel, the land ceases to be considered an agricultural
land and the expenditure does not qualify for capital deduction
as an expenditure on agricultural land.

Where the owner or tenant of agricultural land incurs capital expenditure on farm-works, he is allowed a deduction of 20% of
the expenditure in each of the five years commencing from the
year in which the expenditure is incurred. It therefore implies
that the cost of the land itself is not entitled to any allowance,
but the cost of construction of farm-works. Farm-works are defined in the Second Schedule of the Income Tax Act as meaning
farmhouses, labour quarters, fences, dips, drains, water and electricity supply works other than machinery, windbreaks, and other
works necessary for the proper operation of the farm. It will be
observed that machinery is excluded from the scope of farm-works
because it is entitled to capital allowance in its own right as a machine, the rate of allowance being dependent on the class within
which the particular item of machinery may fall.

If capital expenditure is incurred on construction of a farmhouse
which will be occupied by the owner or tenant of the land, only
one-third of the cost is eligible for capital allowance, i.e. the
20% capital allowance is calculated on one-third of the cost of
the farmhouse. If capital expenditure is incurred on an asset other
than a farmhouse that may be used partly for purposes of husbandry and partly for other purposes (e.g. private use), the Commissioner of Income Tax has the right to restrict the capital
allowance as he may determine to be just and reasonable.

Example 38:

Mudogo, a farmer, incurred the following expenditure in 1976:

	£
Construction of a farmhouse	24,000
Construction of labour quarters	12,000
Construction of cattle dips	2,000
Construction of drains	1,000
Purchase of tractors	36,000

Capital allowance for 1976 will be calculated as follows:

	£
Farmhouse (1/3rd of £24,000)	8,000
Labour quarters	12,000
Dips	2,000
Drains	1,800
Total capital expenditure on *farmworks*	23,800
Capital Allowance on farmworks @ 20% of £23,800	4,760
Wear and Tear Allowance on Tractors @ 37½% of £36,000	13,500
Total Capital Allowance for 1976	18,260

Notes:

(1) In each of the following four years Mr Mudogo will be allowed a capital deduction of £4,760 for farmworks.

(2) Tractors are classified as Machinery Class I and hence entitled to a wear and tear allowance of 37½% of written down value. In the following years this allowance will not be calculated on £36,000 (cost) but on the written down value.

Transfer of Agricultural land

Where a person who was receiving capital allowances transfers the agricultural land to another person:

(a) The amount of deductions, if any, for the year in which the transfer takes place is apportioned between the transferor and transferee in such a manner as the Commissioner of Income Tax may consider to be just and reasonable. In most cases the basis of apportionment is time. Thus if an agricultural land is transferred after three months of commencement of a year, the new owner is granted 75% of the year's capital allowance while the transferor gets only 25% of it.

(b)   In subsequent years the transferee receives the whole of deductions if the whole of the land has been transferred. If he has acquired only part of the land, the Commissioner of Income Tax has the power to determine the basis of apportionment.

Where the interest in agricultural land is a leasehold interest and it comes to an end, then such interest is deemed to have been transferred:

(a)   to the in-coming tenant if he makes payment to the out-going tenant in respect of the assets on that land,
(b)   in any other case, to the owner of the leasehold interest.

CAPITAL ALLOWANCES IN RESPECT OF MINING OPERATIONS

Capital allowances in respect of mining operations are available for capital expenditure incurred on any of the following:

(a)   Searching for, discovery of, testing or winning access to minerals.
(b)   On acquisition of certain rights on or over such deposits other than acquisition from a person who has carried on mining in relation to such deposits.
(c)   Buildings, machinery and other works which would have little or no value to such persons if the mine ceases to be worked.
(d)   On development, general administration and management prior to the commencement of production or during any period of non-production.

An important exception, however, is the cost of land that may be acquired for items listed as (b) and (c) above. The cost of land does not qualify for any capital allowance.

Rate of Capital Allowance

A capital allowance of 40% of the capital expenditure is granted in the first year and of 10% in each of the six subsequent years. Thus the total capital allowance does not exceed the total capital expenditure. If the Commissioner of Income Tax is satisfied that the mining life will not last seven years, he may increase the allowance to such an amount as he may consider just and reasonable, provided always that the total allowance does not exceed total expenditure.

Transfer of Qualifying Assets

If the qualifying assets are sold before the total capital allowance is used up, the apportionment is made between the transferor and transferee on the same basis as listed for agricultural land earlier in this chapter.

INVESTMENT ALLOWANCE

In addition to wear and tear allowance an investment allowance may be claimed for certain fixed assets. This allowance, as stated earlier in this chapter, is granted to provide an incentive to businessmen to invest in capital projects and is allowed only once in the year in which the asset is first used. It is not deducted from the cost of the assets so that it does not affect the calculation of wear and tear allowance.

For the following capital expenditure the rate of investment allowance is 20%:

(a) On the construction of an industrial building used by the owner or a lessee, provided the construction of the building commenced after 1st January 1974.

(b) On purchase and installation of machinery in an industrial building. The allowance would be available irrespective of the fact that the building is owned or leased by the person claiming the capital allowance.

(c) On the building or extension of a certified hotel, provided its construction or extension commenced after 1st January 1974, and on the purchase of machinery to be installed or used solely in the hotel. Investment allowance is not available to hotels built within the limits of municipalities of Nairobi and Mombasa.

(d) On the purchase and installation of machinery after 1st January 1974 in a non-industrial building which is subsequently used for the purposes of an approved business.

It may be pointed out that the investment allowance is granted only in respect of new fixed assets, not on used or second hand assets.

Example 39:

During the year ended 31st December 1976, Simba Manufacturing Co. Ltd. incurred the following capital expenditure:

(a) £1,000 on extension of its factory to accommodate new plant.

(b) £5,000 on purchase of new plant.

(c) £18,000 on construction of new machine shop and a workers' canteen. The factory was built in 1974 at a cost of £30,000.

(d) £4,000 on purchase of two new machines to replace two
     old machines that had a written down value of £600 and
     that were sold for £950.

The written down value of the plant for income tax purposes
was £22,000 on 1st January 1976. New buildings came into use
on 1st July 1976.

Capital Allowance Computation:

		£
(a)	Investment Allowance @ 20% on £18,000	3,600
(b)	Wear and Tear Allowance @ 2½% on original building (£30,000)	750
(c)	Wear and Tear Allowance @ 2½% of new buildings (£18,000) (As the new buildings were built on 1.7.1976, only a half-year's allowance would be claimed)	225
		4,575

Machinery and Plant

(a) Investment allowance @ 20% of £10,000 = £2,000.
     The figure of £10,000 is arrived at as follows:

	£
Purchase of new Plant	5,000
Purchase of new machines	4,000
Cost of extending factory to accommodate new plant	1,000
	10,000

(b) Wear and Tear Allowance:

	£
Written down value on 1.1.1976	22,000
Purchase of new plant (as above)	10,000
	32,000
Less Sale of old Machines	950
	31,050
Wear and Tear Allowance @ 12½% of £31,050	3,881
Written down value on 31.12.1976 (or 1.1.1977)	27,169

£

Summary of Allowances

		£
Industrial Building:	Investment Allowance	3,600
	Wear & Tear Allowance	975
Plant & Machinery:	Investment Allowance	2,000
	Wear & Tear Allowance	3,881
Total Capital Allowance for 1976		10,456

Investment Allowance on Ships

When a resident person carrying on a business of a ship-owner incurs capital expenditure on the purchase of a new ship of more than 495 tons, or on the purchase and subsequent refitting of a used power-driven ship of more than 495 tons, for the purposes of his business, he is allowed to deduct 40% investment allowance of such capital expenditure in the year in which the ship is first used. It will be remembered that ships, being a Class III machinery (as listed in Second Schedule), are also entitled to 12½% wear and tear allowance which is in addition to the investment allowance.

Not more than one investment deduction is allowed in respect of a purchase and refitting of a used ship unless the expenditure on refitting is more than 25% of the total capital expenditure incurred.

Where a ship in respect of which an investment allowance has been given is sold within a period of five years from the end of the year in which the investment allowance was given, the allowance is withdrawn and treated as income of the vendor for the year in which the sale takes place.

QUESTIONS

1. Why is depreciation not allowed as an expense deductible from gross profit?
2. List the capital allowances available on industrial building.
3. How would you define an investment allowance? Why is it granted?
4. What is the main difference between a wear and tear allowance and a depreciation charge?
5. What is meant by the following terms?
   (a) Balancing Charge
   (b) Balancing Allowance
   (c) An industrial building

    (d)   Three classes of machinery.

6. How is a balancing charge or allowance treated in books if only a part of the asset is sold?

7. In what respects is an investment allowance different from other capital allowance(s)?

8. How is a balancing allowance treated if:
    (a)   no new asset is bought to replace the old asset?
    (b)   a new asset is bought to replace the old asset?

9. How is a balancing charge treated in the circumstances listed under Question 8?

10. List the capital allowance available to farmers.

11. List the capital allowances available to shipowners.

12. List the capital allowances available to traders.

13. What is a wear and tear schedule?

14. Prepare a wear and tear schedule from the following information:

       Written down value of motor vehicle, 1.1.1978, £24,200
       Cost of new vehicles bought in 1978, £4,000
       Written down value of furniture on 1.1.1978, £3,200
       Written down value of industrial building on 1.1.1978, £40,000
       Cost of new furniture bought in 1978, £1,200.

    No fixed asset was sold during the year.

15. Calculate capital allowances from the following information:

	£
Written down values on 31.12.1977	
Motor vehicles (six)	5,600
Tractors and Harvesters (three)	42,500
Plant and Machinery	18,360
Furniture and Fittings	8,800
Additions during 1978	
One motor vehicle	2,600
Plant and Machinery	4,000
One tractor	8,400
Disposals during the year 1978	
One motor vehicle	800
All furniture and fittings	5,000

16. Calculate capital allowances from the following information:

	£
Written down values on 1.1.1978	
Land and Buildings (industrial)	25,000
Plant and Machinery	24,800
Furniture	2,600

	£
Additions during 1978	
Construction of new factory	20,000
Purchase of new plant for new factory	32,000
Disposals during the year	
Plant and Machinery	6,000
All furniture	3,000

The cost of land, included in land and buildings, is £5,000.

17. From the following information calculate the capital allowances claimable by Joseph Barassa, a farmer, for 1978:

	£
Written down values on 1.1.1978	
Farmhouse	10,000
Tractors (three)	16,400
Pick up vehicle (one)	1,600
Sundry Tools and Furniture	2,200
During 1978 he:	
built a new cattle dip	1,000
built two labour quarters	2,800
bought one tractor	6,200
sold the pick up vehicle	1,000
sold all sundry tools and furniture	2,400
bought a truck with a trailor	7,800

18. Wananchi Shipping Co. Ltd. carries on the business of a ship-owner. On 1st January 1978 they had three ships, all of over 800 tons, with a written down value of £200,000. One of the ships that they had bought in 1976 for £120,000 was sold in 1978 for £100,000. In the same year they also bought another ship, also over 800 tons, for £150,000.
Calculate the amount of capital allowances that the company can claim in 1978.

Chapter Eight

INCOME FROM PROFESSIONS

WHO IS A PROFESSIONAL PERSON?

A professional person is one who carries on, whether alone or in partnership, one of the professions listed in the Fifth Schedule of the Income Tax Act, and has the necessary qualifications to do so. The Schedule lists the following professions and qualifications:

Profession	Qualifications
1. Medical	Any person who is registered as a Medical Practitioner under the Medical Practitioners and Dentists Act (Cap. 253).
2. Dental	Any person who is registered as a Dentist under the Medical Practitioners and Dentists Act (Cap. 253).
3. Legal	Any person who is an Advocate within the meaning of the Advocates Act (Cap. 16).
4. Surveyors (a) Land Surveyor	Any person licensed as a Surveyor under the Survey Act (Cap. 299).
(b) Surveyor	Any person who is a fellow or professional associate of the Royal Institution of Chartered Surveyors.
5. Architects or Quantity Surveyor	Any person who is registered as an Architect or Quantity Surveyor under the Architects or Quantity Surveyors Act. (Cap. 525).
6. Veterinary Surgeons	Any person who is registered or licensed as a Veterinary Surgeon under the Veterinary Surgeons Act (Cap. 366).
7. Engineers	Any person who is registered under the Engineers Registration Act (Cap. 530).

8. Accountants	Any member of any of the professional bodies specified in the first column of the Schedule to the Accountants (Designation) Act (Cap. 524).

ALLOWABLE EXPENSES

In addition to the expenses usually allowable to all business, as listed on pages 52-54 in Chapter Six, a professional person is permitted to charge the following to his Profit and Loss Account for the purpose of determining income for tax computation.

(a) A housing deduction equal to 15% of the gains or profits from his profession or Shs. 14,000 whichever is the less.

(b) Any subscriptions paid to a professional body to retain his name on its register.

Example 40:

J. Kitabu is a qualified practising accountant. The following information is extracted from his books for the year ended 31st December 1978:

		£
Income:	Fees	7,100
	Part-time teaching	200
Expenditure:	Rent	600
	Secretary's salary	1,200
	Stationery	75
	Newspapers and periodicals	25
	Car running expenses	450
	General office expenses (all allowable)	300
	Professional subscriptions	20
	Business entertainment	150
	Donations to charities	20
	Purchase of new office furniture	800

Additional information

(a) On 1st January 1978 the written down value of his car was £960 and of office furniture and fittings £600. It has been agreed with the Income Tax Department that one-third of the total use of car is for private purposes.

(b) He pays 10% interest on a £9,000 bank loan obtained to purchase the house in which he lives.

(c) He pays £200 per annum for insurance premium on a policy on his life that secures a capital sum on death payable in Kenya.

(d) He is married.

His tax liability for 1978 will be calculated as follows:

	£	£
Income from Profession: Fees		7,100
Less *Expenses on Profession*		
Rent	600	
Secretary's Salary	1,200	
Stationery	75	
Newspapers and periodicals	25	
Car running expenses (2/3rd of £450)	300	
General Office Expenses	300	
Professional subscriptions	20	
Business entertainment	150	2,670
Net Income from Profession		4,430
Less *Housing Deduction*		
15% of net income from profession, £4,430 or £700, whichever is the less.		664
		3,766
Add *Other Income*		
Part-time Teaching		200
		3,966
Less *Wear and Tear Allowance*		
Furniture 12½% of (£600 + 800)	175	
Motor Car 2/3rd of 25% of £960	160	
Other Expenses		
Interest on Bank Loan: 10% on £9,000	900	1,235
Net Taxable Income		2,271

Tax Computation	Shs.
On £1,200 @ 2/= per £	2,400
On £1,200 @ 3/= per £	3,600
On £ 331 @ 5/= per £	1,655
	7,655

Less: Family Relief	1,680	
Insurance Relief: 10% of 4,000	400	2,080
Tax Liability		5,575

Note that 15% housing deduction is calculated on his net professional income, excluding any other income. Again, wear and tear allowance is a capital allowance and not an expense. Interest on loan for house is also not considered a 'professional expense'.

QUESTIONS

1. Who is a professional person?
2. List the deductions allowable to a professional person that are not allowable to a trader.
3. What is a housing deduction allowable to a professional person equal to?
4. P. Painless, a practising doctor, drew up the following revenue account for 1978:

Revenue Account for 1978

	£	£
Fees for services rendered		8,190
Income from overseas investments		2,000
		10,190
Less *Expenses*		
Nurses and attendants' wages	2,800	
Car running expenses	480	
Light, heat and Postage (surgery)	250	
Telephone (house and surgery)	180	
Bank charges	20	
Stationery	40	
Subscription to Medical Association	10	
Rent and Rates	900	
Donation to charities	200	
Salary to house servant	210	
General Expenses (all allowable)	430	
		5,520
Net Income		4,670

Mrs Painless works as a secretary with an insurance company and earns a monthly salary of £80. In July 1978 she had received a bonus of £100 from her employers. PAYE deducted from her pay for the year was 1,920. They have no children. They have a joint life insurance policy on which premium is paid @ Shs. 4,000 p.a. 40% of the car running expenses and 60% of telephone expenses are attributeable to personal and private use.

Calculate Dr. Painless's income tax liability for 1978.

Chapter Nine

INCOME OF SPECIAL BUSINESSES

SPECIAL BUSINESSES

Special businesses is not a legal term. It is being used in this chapter specifically to refer to such business establishments whose profit (or net income) cannot usually be ascertained in the same way as that of a trading or a manufacturing business, or a profession. Some of these businesses are insurance companies, unit trusts, members clubs and trade associations, etc. It is not possible for a book of this nature to list or discuss every type of business but an attempt is being made to cover the more important of them.

INSURANCE COMPANIES

If an insurance company carries on life insurance business together with other type(s) of insurance business, the life insurance business is treated as a separate business from any other class of insurance business. This distinction is necessary because of great difference in the nature of life and general insurance businesses.

General Insurance Business

Gains or profits for any year of income from insurance business other than a life insurance business are ascertained as follows:

Income

- (a) The amount of gross premiums received, less any refunds made.
- (b) The amount of any other income from such business including any commission or expense allowance received, any income derived from investments held in connection with general insurance business.

Deductions

- (a) The amount of claims admitted less amounts recovered under re-insurance.
- (b) Agency expenses.
- (c) Other allowable expenses under the Income Tax Act. These

include such items that are allowable to all businesses, e.g. staff salaries, rent, rates, reasonable advertising, etc.

(d) A reserve for unexpired risks. This reserve may be created at a reasonable percentage of premiums received by the insurance company. However, from this reserve must be *deducted* the amount of any reserve for unexpired risk created at the end of previous year. Thus if an insurance company received premiums totalling £300,000 in 1976 and £410,000 in 1977 and it creates a 40% reserve for unexpired risks, the amount allowable for deduction from 1977 income will be calculated as follows:

Reserve created on 31.12.1976	
@ 40% of £300,000	£120,000
Reserve created on 31.12.1977	
@ 40% of £410,000	£164,000
	£ 42,000

Life Insurance Business

The gains or profits of a life insurance business are taken to be the sum of the following:

(a) The amount of the investment income of its life insurance fund less the expenses of management (including commission), and

(b) The amount of any interest paid by the company from its annuity fund on surrender of policies or on the return of premiums, other than any such interest which relates to premiums paid under a registered annuity contract, registered trust scheme, registered pension scheme or fund.

It is important to note that whereas in a general insurance business the premiums received constitute the bulk of the insurance company's income, in a life insurance business the premiums received are not considered an income at all. Life insurance companies invest the premiums received in profitable securities and it is the income received from such investments that forms the major part of their income.

UNIT TRUSTS

A unit trust is a group of people who accept money from other persons and invest it in profitable securities. Any amount distributed by the manager or trustee to unit holders is considered a dividend and treated as a part of the income of the unit-holders.

Any income of the unit trust that is not distributed is also deemed to be dividend and is taxable. A unit holder pays tax on such part of the undistributed income of the unit trust as his holding is of the total holding of the trust. Thus if a unit trust has a total of 100,000 units and a certain unit-holder holds 1,000 of them, such unit holder will be taxed on 1% of the income retained by the unit trust.

MEMBERS' CLUBS AND TRADE ASSOCIATIONS

A body of persons which carries on a members' club is considered to be carrying on a business and its income (including entrance fees, subscriptions, donations) is considered as income of the business and hence taxable. However, if 75% or more of the club's income is received from its members then the club is not deemed to be a business and its income (except investment income) is exempt from tax. If the club makes a loss, the loss cannot be offset against investment income.

A trade association can choose to have its income considered as business income and be charged tax on it. In this case the whole of the income (less expenses) will be taxed but if the trade association incurs a loss, the loss can be offset against investment income.

NON-RESIDENT BUSINESSES

If a non-resident person (or company) carries on a business in Kenya through a permanent establishment here, the profits or gains of the permanent establishment would be calculated without deducting any fees, royalties, interest or management expenses paid by the establishment to the non-resident person.

Any profits earned by a non-resident business based in Kenya would be taxed in Kenya even if they arise from contracts outside Kenya. No deduction is allowed on expenditure incurred outside Partner States unless the Commissioner of Income Tax determines that adequate consideration has been given. In particular no deduction is allowed for the following expenses incurred outside Kenya:

(a)   Remuneration of a non-resident director in excess of 5% of the business's income (before calculating the salary), or £1,250 whichever is the greater if the directors have a controlling interest in the company. Again not more than £7,500 is allowed for remuneration of all such directors. The limit of £1,250 does not apply if the director is a whole-time service director.

(b) Executive and general administration expenses except to the extent that Commissioner of Income Tax may determine to be just and reasonable. This provision is made in the law to avoid Kenya branches of over-seas companies paying excessive sums as their contribution to their head offices' administration overheads.

QUESTIONS

1. Describe the procedure for determining chargeable profits of a life insurance company.
2. Describe the procedure for determining chargeable profits of a general insurance company.
3. If an insurance company transacts both life and general insurance business, how would its chargeable profit be determined?
4. What is a unit trust? How is the income of a unit trust determined.
5. What status is enjoyed by members' clubs and trade associations as far as determining their tax liability is concerned?
6. How are non-resident businesses taxed?
7. How would be the profits of a branch in Kenya of a non-Kenyan company be ascertained? What items are allowable deductions and what items are not allowable deductions for such branches?

Chapter Ten

CORPORATION TAX

WHO PAYS CORPORATION TAX?

Section 34 of the Income Tax Act states that the income of persons other than individuals will be taxed at Corporation Tax rates. In this case the term 'persons other than individuals' is intended to include not only joint stock companies but also trade associations and members clubs who may elect to declare their establishment a business. The term however excludes partnerships as a business run by partners does not have an entity of its own.

Non-resident companies are chargeable to Corporation Tax only if they carry on a trade (or business) in Kenya through a branch or agency, and then only in respect of the profits attributable to the branch or agency.

CORPORATION TAX RATES

These rates are announced in the annual Budget proposals. The following rates are applicable at present:

Resident Companies	45%
Non-resident Companies	52½%
Life Insurance Companies	40%
Mining Companies	
for the first 5 years	27½%
thereafter	45%

COMPUTATION OF PROFITS OF A COMPANY

The method of arriving at an adjusted net profit is the same for companies as that for sole traders and partnerships. The following items should, however, be added to the list of items allowable and items not allowable as a deduction for the purpose of ascertaining net profit for tax computation:

(a) *Deductions Allowable*

Directors Fees, unless paid to members of the family and not laid out wholly and exclusively for the purposes of the trade, e.g. any fees paid to an infant who may have been appointed a director of a family controlled private company.

(b) *Deductions Not Allowable*

   (1) Loans made to directors which may prove irrecoverable.
   (2) Defalcations by a director.
   (3) Formation expenses.
   (4) Cost of raising share capital, discount on shares and debentures, underwriting commission for issue of shares, etc.
   (5) Legal Expenses in respect of a proposed increase in capital.
   (6) Dividends and other distributions from profits.
   (7) Payment of Corporation Tax.
   (8) Interest on arrears of Corporation Tax.

(c) *Income from Dividends Received*

   If a company receives dividends and other distributions from another company the amount so received is treated as a part of the receiving company's income, and is hence taxable. However, if the company that receives dividends holds 12½% or more of the share capital of the company that pays dividends, the dividend so received will not be taxable for the receiving company. Thus if Nairobi Co. Ltd. holds 20% of the share capital of Thika Co. Ltd., any dividends declared by Thika Co. Ltd. and received by Nairobi Co. Ltd. will not be treated as a taxable income of Nairobi Co. Ltd.

WITHHOLDING TAX

Companies must deduct withholding tax, at prevailing rates, from any dividends declared by them, and pay only the net amount to their shareholders. Withholding Tax so deducted must be paid over to the Collector of Income Tax in about the same manner an employer is required to remit any tax he has deducted from his employees' emoluments under P.A.Y.E. system. However if the dividend payable to any individual shareholder does not exceed Shs. 150, the amount may be paid gross, i.e. without deducting withholding tax.

Withholding tax must also be deducted from any interest (e.g. on debentures) paid by a company. However, if the amount of interest payable to any one person does not exceed Shs. 200, the amount may be paid gross.

At present the withholding tax rate is 15% of dividends and 12½% of interest payments.

WITHHOLDING TAX ON DIVIDENDS RECEIVED

If a company receives dividends or interest out of which withholding tax has already been deducted, the company can offset such deduction from its own Corporation Tax liability and pay the net amount to the Collector of Income Tax.

Example 41:

The accounts of Kakamego Co. Ltd. show the following results for the year 1977:

Adjusted Trading Profit for Tax purposes	£40,000
Dividends Received from other Companies in which less than 12½% of their shares are held (included in profit)	£ 2,550 (net)
Corporation Tax @ 45% of £40,000	£18,000

Net Corporation Tax liability will be calculated as follows:

Step 1: Assess the amount deducted from dividends received.
At present withholding tax rate is 15% of gross amount.

$$\text{Gross Amount} = £2,550 \times \frac{100}{85} = £3,000$$

Tax Deducted = £3,000 less £2,550 = £450.

Step 2: Corporation Tax	£18,000
Less Withholding Tax on Dividends Received	450
Net Corporation Tax Due	17,550

CAPITAL ALLOWANCES

Capital allowances permissible to sole traders and partnerships are also available to companies. Capital Allowances are treated as expenses when calculating net profit for tax purposes.

Example 42:

The following is a summary of the Profit and Loss Account for the year ended 31st December 1975 of Impo Expo Co. Ltd.:

Profit and Loss Account

	£		£
Salaries	9,600	Gross Profit	28,200
Rates and Insurance	1,200	Rent	750
Light and Heat	1,314	Investment Income	1,700
Doubtful Debts	25	Profit on sale of	
General Expenses	248	Machinery	90

	£	£
Legal charges	50	
Audit Fees	84	
Directors' Fees	8,500	
Motor Van:		
Running Expenses	1,200	
Dpreciation	220	
Net Profit before Tax	8,299	
	30,740	30,740

Notes

(1) Legal charges were incurred during an abortive attempt to obtain larger premises.

(2) General Expenses include:
    Subscriptions paid to a trade association, £15
    Donations to a local hospital, £10
    Christmas gifts in kind to junior members of staff, £40
    Bank interest on overdraft, £5
    Parking fine, £3
    Loss on sale of a motor van, £37.

(3) The charge for doubtful debts represents the amount required to bring the provisions for doubtful debts to 5% of debtors on 31st December 1975.

(4) The company owned three motor vehicles on 1st January 1975 with a written down value of £600. All three vehicles were sold on 1st October 1975 for £560.

(5) In September 1975 two second-hand vans and one new van were bought for £1,216 and £800 respectively.

(6) Investment income consists of:

	£
Interest on Tax Reserve certificates	200
Debenture Interest (gross)	400
Dividends on ordinary shares of a Kenya company in which Impo Expo Ltd. holds 15% of the ordinary share capital (gross)	1,100
	1,700

(7) The company had machinery of a written down value for tax purposes of £200 on 1st January 1975. In March 1975 it was sold for £230.

Calculate the corporation tax liability of the company for the year ended 31st December 1975.

Computation of Adjusted Net Profit

	£	£
Net Profit as per accounts		8,299
Add Expenses Not Allowable		
Depreciation		220
Legal Charges		50
Donations		10
Parking Fines		3
Loss on sale of motor vans		37
Doubtful Debts Provision		25
		8,644
Less		
Profit on sale of machinery	90	
Investment Income:		
Dividends not taxable	1,100	
Interest on Tax Reserve Certificates	200	
Wear & Tear Allowance (see note below)	484	
		1,874
Taxable Profit		6,770
Corporation Tax on £6,770 @ 45%		3,096
Less: Withholding Tax on Debenture Interest	50	
Withholding Tax on Dividends	165	
		215
Net Corporation Tax Liability		2,881

Notes:

(1) Notice that loss on sale of motor vehicles is shown as £37 in the Profit and Loss Account, whereas the difference between the written down value (for tax purpose) and the amount received on disposal is £40 (£600 - 560). Can you guess the reason? It is possible that the written down value in the books of accounts may not be the same as the written down value for tax purposes. Similarly profit on sale of machinery as per books of accounts is given at £90 whereas Balancing Charge for tax purposes amounts to only £30. See Note 2 for further details.

(2) Written down value of Machinery (1.1.1975):   £200
     Amount realised on its disposal   230

     Balancing Charge deductible from wear and tear   £ 30
     allowance on other fixed assets

(3) Wear and Tear Allowance on Motor Vehicles is calculated as follows:

	£
Written down Value on 1.1.1975	600
Add: New purchases	2,016
	2,616
Less: Amount realised on disposal	560
Written down value on 31.12.1975	2,056
Wear & Tear Allowance @ 25% of £2,056	514
Less: Balancing Charge on Machinery	30
Wear & Tear Allowance shown in statement above	484

(4) Withholding Tax on debenture interest received is calculated at 12½% and on dividends at 15%. Though there is no mention in the question whether the interest and dividends were received gross or net, we must assume that withholding tax has already been deducted. Reason: It is mandatory for any company paying interest in excess of Shs. 200, or dividend in excess of Shs. 150, to any one person, to deduct withholding tax, and in this example the amounts received were far in excess of these amounts.

(5) Interest received on Tax Reserve Certificates is exempt from tax. See First Schedule (Part I) of the Income Tax Act.

AVOIDANCE OF TAX LIABILITY BY NON-DISTRIBUTION OF DIVIDENDS

Private companies are usually controlled by their directors who in most cases hold all or majority of the share capital. Such directors may, in order to reduce their personal tax liability, decide not to declare any dividends, or to declare very low dividends. Dividends paid to shareholders are a taxable income to them and if no or very little dividends are paid, the shareholders will be liable to no or very little income tax. The directors can, of course, draw money for their personal needs from the company by way of loans (which are not considered an income to them) and never repay these loans.

Section 24 of the Income Tax Act effectively checks this malpractice. It empowers the Commissioner of Income Tax to determine the amount of distribution that could be made without prejudice to the requirements of the company's financial needs. If the actual distribution made by the company is less than the amount determined by the Commissioner, the difference is *deemed* to have been distributed, and hence a part of the income of the shareholders. We will call this difference 'notional distribution'. Two points need particular attention here. Firstly, notional distribution is only *deemed to have been made.* This means that it is not obligatory for the company to actually distribute an additional amount to its shareholders. Secondly, the notional dividends should be added to the income of shareholders who would be liable to pay income tax on them. But the income tax is payable by the shareholders. It follows that notional distribution does not bring any additional tax liability to the company but to the individual shareholders.

The additional notional distribution is deemed to be made twelve months after the end of the company's accounting year. The company may be required by the Commissioner of Income Tax to pay income tax attributable to notional dividends to the Collector of Income Tax. But as this tax is really the liability of the shareholders, the Company has the right to recover it from its shareholders.

If a company can prove to the satisfaction of the Commissioner of Income Tax that it is unable to distribute the required amount of the profits because of lack of liquid funds, firm capital commitments, etc., the Commissioner may not enforce the above provision.

If the Commissioner of Income Tax directs an additional notional distribution but the company does not actually pay the dividends, it will still be required to pay tax that would be due from shareholders if the dividends had been paid. If in a later year these dividends are actually paid the shareholders would not be required to pay further income tax at the time of distribution of dividends.

A company can retain a part of its trading profits but must distribute all of its income from interest, capital gains and investments.

Example 43:

Kisumu Trading Co. Ltd. is a private company whose entire share capital is held equally by James Omolo and Peter Onyango. Both of them are directors of the company. James Omolo is married and has an insurance policy on his life for which he pays an annual premium of Shs. 5,000. Peter Onyango is single but maintains a child under 16 years of age.

The company made the following adjusted profits in 1978:

	£
Trading Profit	5,000
Interest and capital gains	2,500
Dividends from Maseno Co. Ltd. (gross)	2,500

Kisumu Co. Ltd. holds 30% of the share capital of Maseno Co. Ltd. The company pays (or proposes to pay) a dividend of 20% on its ordinary share capital that consists of 10,000 shares of £1 each. The company has no other form of share capital. Commissioner of Income Tax determines that 40% of the trading income should be distributed.

James Omolo earned £1,670 from other sources and Peter Onyango had a net income of £1,200 as rents from his personal property.

Corporation Tax Liability and notional dividends of the Company will be calculated as follows:

	Trading Profit	Interest and Capital Gains	Dividends from Maseno Co. Ltd.	Total
	£	£	£	£
Income	5,000	2,500	2,500	10,000
Corporation Tax (45%)	2,250	1,125	———	3,375
Available for Distribution	2,750	1,375	2,500	6,625
Retention (60%)	1,650	———	———	1,650
To be distributed	1,100	1,375	2,500	4,975
Proposed Dividends (20% of £10,000)				2,000
				2,975

Note

No corporation Tax is charged on dividends from Maseno Co. Ltd. as Kisumu Co. Ltd. holds more than 12½% of the share capital of Maseno Co. Ltd.

Income Tax Liability of James Omolo and Peter Onyango will be calculated as follows:

	James Omolo	Peter Onyango
	£	£
Income from other sources	1,670	1,200
Dividends from Kisumu Co. Ltd.	1,000	1,000
Actual Income	2,670	2,200

	James Omolo £	Peter Onyango £
Actual Income b/f	2,670	2,200
Notional Dividends	1,487	1,487
Taxable Income	4,157	3,687

Notes

(1) Dividends from Kisumu Co. Ltd. were £2,000, divided equally between Omolo and Onyango.

(2) Notional Dividends are calculated as ½ of £2,975.

Calculation of Income Tax	*J. Omolo* Shs.	*P. Onyango* Shs.
On first £1,200 @ 2/= per £	2,400	2,400
On next £1,200 @ 3/= per £	3,600	3,600
On next £1,200 @ 5/= per £	6,000	6,000
On next £ 557 (Omolo), £87 (Onyango) @ 7/=	3,899	609
	15,899	12,609

J. Omolo: Gross Tax		15,899
Less: Family Relief	1,680	
Insurance Relief (maximum)	480	2,160
Net Income Tax		13,739

P. Onyango: Gross Tax		12,609
Less: Single Relief (Special)		720
Net Income Tax		11,889

Note

If the Commissioner of Income Tax directs Kisumu Co. Ltd. to remit income tax payable by shareholders on notional dividends it will be calculated as follows:

	Omolo Shs.	*Onyango* Shs.
Gross Tax	15,899	12,609
Less: Tax attributeable to income excluding notional dividends	7,350	5,400
Tax Attributeable to Notional Dividends	8,549	7,209

You will notice that though both the shareholders were apportioned the same amount of notional dividends, the amount of tax attributeable to such dividends is different in each case. The reason: Notional dividends are treated as top slice of an individual's income and taxed accordingly. Hence Mr Omolo, who is in a higher tax bracket due to larger income from other sources, will pay higher amount of income tax on notional dividends than Onyango whose income from other sources is smaller and hence in a lower tax bracket.

To avoid complications as those that arise from keeping a distinction between notional and actual distributions, a private company may, before making any distributions, inquire from the Commissioner of Income Tax whether the distribution it proposes to make is sufficient. The Commissioner of Income Tax would, after making appropriate enquiries, advise the Company of what he considers to be a reasonable distribution. The Company would then be able to decide whether to pay the dividends as suggested by the Commissioner and have no problems of keeping notional distribution in its books, or to pay the amount it originally proposed and to pay income tax due from shareholders on notional distribution to the Collector of Income Tax and proceed to recover such a tax from its shareholders.

The Commissioner of Income Tax will not intervene in distribution of dividends in the cases of the following companies:

(a)   Public Companies
(b)   A private company controlled by a public company
(c)   Any company controlled directly or indirectly by the government.

QUESTIONS

1.   Who is liable to corporation tax? Is a limited partner in a partnership business liable to corporation tax?
2.   List the corporation tax rates applicable to the different types of companies.
3.   List the items allowable to a company that are usually not allowable to other businessmen.
4.   If a company holds less than 12½% of the share capital of another company, how are the dividends paid by the 'subsidiary company' treated in the books of the holding company'?
6.   What are notional dividends?
7.   Under what circumstances may the Commissioner of Income

Tax interfere into the dividend policy of a private company?
8. Notional dividends do not bring an additional tax liability to a company. Is this statement true or false? Give reasons.
9. List the type of companies whose dividend policy cannot be interfered with by the Commissioner of Income Tax.
10. Mr Ngari and Mr Luka are directors of a private company, Greengardens Limited. The company made the following incomes in 1978:

	£
Trading Profit	12,400
Income from local investments (gross)	1,000
Dividends received from Bluefarms Ltd. (gross)	2,500

Greengardens Ltd. holds 20% of the ordinary share capital of Bluefarms Ltd. No withholding tax has been deducted from investment income or dividends received from Bluefarms Ltd.

Greengardens Ltd. has proposed and paid a dividend of 20% on its share capital of £25,000. The Commissioner of Income Tax feels that at least 75% of the trading profit and the whole of other incomes should be distributed as dividends.

Mr Ngari is married and pays insurance premium of £500 per year.

He has no other source of income.

Mr Luka is also married. Mrs Luka earns a salary of £1,200 per annum while Mr Luka is in receipt of a pension of £600 per annum. Mr & Mrs Luka live in a house provided by Mrs Luka's employers. PAYE deducted from her salary in 1978 was Shs. 2,400.

Calculate the company's Corporation Tax liability, and the tax liability of Mr Ngari and Mr Luka.

Chapter Eleven

WITHHOLDING TAX, SET-OFF OF TAX AND DOUBLE TAXATION

WITHHOLDING TAX

Wherever possible the Government tries to deduct tax before the income reaches the person to whom it belongs. For example in the case of income from employment, employers are directed to deduct income tax on employees' salaries before paying them at the end of each month. Similar principles apply to various other payments made to resident persons. The person making certain types of payments is required to withhold tax and pay the net amount only to the person whom it belongs. The tax so withheld should be paid over to the Collector of Income Tax within a stipulated period. The tax so withheld is termed as 'Withholding Tax'. It should be noted that withholding tax is not a special tax (like income tax or corporation tax or sales tax) but a method of deducting income tax on certain payments made to resident persons.

A person who receives any income from which withholding tax has been deducted is required to show the gross amount as an income in his annual tax return, but he will be given credit for the tax withheld.

RATES OF WITHHOLDING TAX

The following rates are applicable at present:

(a) In respect of any dividends, 15% of the amount payable. No withholding tax should, however, be deducted if the amount payable is less than Shs. 150.

(b) In respect of any interest, 12½% of the gross amount payable. Again, no withholding tax should be deducted if the amount payable is less than Shs. 200.

(c) In respect of any commission paid by an insurance company to any individual for the provision of insurance cover to any person, 15% of the gross amount payable.

It should be noted that withholding tax is *not* intended to be the total tax due on the amounts received as above. Any income from which withholding tax has been deducted is treated in the same manner as any other income (e.g. from employment). At the end of a year of income, all incomes (including those against which withholding tax has been deducted) should be shown in the tax return. Income Tax is then calculated on the total income. From the tax so calculated will be deducted any withholding tax and any tax deducted by way of P.A.Y.E., to arrive at the net tax due.

Example 44:

George Gethi is an insurance agent. During 1978 he received the following sums:

Salary (gross)	£800
Insurance Commission (net)	£850

Mr Gethi is single. His employer had deducted PAYE of Shs. 1,000 from his salary.

His tax liability will be computed as follows:

Step 1: Calculate the amount of gross insurance commission:

$$£850 \times \frac{100}{85} = £1,000.$$

Step 2: Calculate the amount of withholding tax on commission. Gross Amount less Net Amount received = Withholding Tax £1,000 - £850 = £150 or Shs. 3,000.

Step 3: Calculate his total income:

	£
Salary	800
Insurance Commission	1,000
Total Income	1,800

Step 4: Calculate tax on total income:

		Shs.
On £1,200 @ 2/= per £		2,400
On £ 600 @ 3/= per £		1,800
On £1,800		4,200
Less: Single Relief	600	
P.A.Y.E.	1,000	
Withholding Tax	3,000	4,600
Tax to be refunded to Gethi		400

Note: In the above example the withholding tax has proved to be greater than the income tax actually attributeable to income from insurance commissions. But if the salary of Mr Gethi were in a higher tax bracket, it may well have been the case that withholding tax would prove insufficient. Study the following example.

Example 45:

Basic facts as for the above example but now assume that Mr Gethi's income from emoluments was £3,200 on which a total of Shs. 9,400 had been deducted. Now calculate his tax liability.

Total Income would be £3,200 + £1,000 = £4,200.

		Shs.
Tax on £1,200 @ 2/= per £		2,400
£1,200 @ 3/= per £		3,600
£1,200 @ 5/= per £		6,000
£ 600 @ 7/= per £		4,200
Tax on £4,200		16,200
Less: Single Relief	600	
P.A.Y.E.	9,400	
Withholding Tax	3,000	
		13,000
Tax still due from Mr Gethi		3,200

WITHHOLDING TAX ON SALE OF PROPERTY

This is discussed in Chapter on Capital Gains Tax.

PAYMENT OF WITHHOLDING TAX TO THE COLLECTOR

Any person who deducts withholding tax must, within 30 days of making the deduction, take the following steps:

1. Remit the amount so deducted to the Collector of Income Tax with the following details:
   (a) The amount of payment
   (b) The amount of tax deducted
   (c) The name and address of the person to whom the payment was made
   (d) The nature of payment, i.e. whether it is dividend, interest, insurance commission, etc.
2. Furnish the person to whom the payment was made with a certificate stating the amount and nature of payment and the amount of tax deducted.

If any person who is required to deduct withholding tax at appropriate rate, fails to remit the amount of any deduction to the Collector of Income Tax within 30 days of the date of payment, the Commissioner of Income Tax would hold that person responsible as if the tax was due from and payable by him.

TAX DEDUCTION FROM PAYMENTS TO NON-RESIDENTS

Withholding tax applies to resident persons only. In the case of non-resident persons who may receive sums of money from Kenya the situation is slightly different. In this case the tax to be deducted represents total tax due on that payment. Compare this with the paragraph given under 'Rates of Withholding Tax' on page 111. The following rates of tax apply to payments made to non-resident persons:

(a)   Any management or professional fees, 20%
(b)   Any rent, premium or like consideration for the use of or occupation of property, 30%
(c)   Any royalty, 20%
(d)   dividends, 15%
(e)   interest, 12½%
(f)   any pension or retirement annuity, 5%
(g)   any fees paid for any appearance at, or performance in, any place for the purpose of entertaining, instructing, taking part in any sporting event or otherwise diverting an audience, 20%.
(h)   any fees paid for any activity by way of supporting, assisting or arranging any appearance or performance mentioned in (g) above, 20%.

The Act maintains a distinction between a non-resident person and a person residing in Partner States (i.e. in Tanzania or Uganda) but at present rates applicable are the same for both of them, i.e. for non-residents and persons residing in Partner States.

Example 46:

Mr Rocker, a well known entertainer from United Kingdom was engaged by Blue Sea Hotel for a period of 10 days. Under the agreement between them, Mr Rocker was to receive a daily allowance of Shs. 500 and a fee of Shs. 2,000 for every performance. He made a total of five performances in 10 days.
Calculation of the amount due to Mr Rocker:

	Shs.
Daily Allowance 500/= x 10	5,000
Performance Fees 2,000/= x 5	10,000
Gross Amount Due	15,000

	Shs.
Gross Amount Due b/f	15,000
Less Tax @ 20%	3,000
Net Amount to be paid to Mr Rocker	12,000

Blue Sea Hotel should pay Shs. 12,000 to Mr Rocker and issue him with a certificate stating that they have deducted Shs. 3,000 from the amounts due to him. They must also remit Shs. 3,000 to the Collector of Income Tax within 30 days of making the payment to Mr Rocker.

SET-OFF OF TAX

Section 39 of the Income Tax Act specifies that any tax which has been deducted at source shall be deemed to have been paid by the person chargeable and shall be off-set for the purpose of collection against the tax charged on such person. In simpler terms, any tax deducted from income at source, e.g. by way of P.A.Y.E. or withholding tax, is deductible from the tax liability of a person which is, in case of resident persons, calculated at the end of a year of income. Refer to the Example on page 112 where Mr Gethi's tax liability amounted to Shs. 16,200 from which were deducted the amounts of tax paid by way of P.A.Y.E. and withholding tax, to arrive at the net tax liability. In the case of Example on page 112, the total tax liability exceeded the amount of tax deducted at source by way of P.A.Y.E. and withholding tax and the excess was refundable to person chargeable.

DOUBLE TAXATION RELIEF

Kenya has Double Taxation Relief agreements with certain countries notably members of East African Community. If a person resident in Kenya who is chargeable to tax derives any income from a country with which Kenya has a Double Taxation Relief Agreement, on which tax has been deducted in that country, he will be given credit for the tax so deducted provided:

(a) he can prove that the tax was actually deducted in that country.

(b) the tax deducted in that country is not more than the tax that he would have paid in Kenya if he had been wholly charged in Kenya. In case the tax deducted in a country with which Kenya has a Double Taxation agreement is more than the tax that the chargeable person would have paid in Kenya, the tax credit given will be restricted to the tax that he would have paid in Kenya on such income.

Procedure of Computing Tax Credit

(a) Compute tax liability *without* income received from a country with which a double taxation agreement exists.

(b) Compute tax liability on total income *including* foreign income.

(c) The excess of (b) over (a) is the maximum amount of Tax Credit that can be allowed to be deducted from total tax liability.

Example 47:

Mr Njoroge earned £2,000 from Kenya and £500 from Tanzania in 1978. He paid Shs. 1,000 by way of tax deducted at source on Tanzanian income. Compute his net tax liability in Kenya assuming that he is a resident of Kenya.

Step 1: *Tax on income excluding income from Tanzania*

	Shs.
On £1,200 @ 2/- per £	2,400
On £ 800 @ 3/- per £	2,400
On £2,000	4,800

Step 2: *Tax on income including income from Tanzania*

	Shs.
On £1,200 @ 2/- per £	2,400
On £1,200 @ 3/- per £	3,600
On £ 100 @ 5/- per £	500
On £2,500	6,500

Step 3: *Net Tax Liability in Kenya*

	Shs.
Tax on total income (including Tanzanian income)	6,500
Less Tax deducted in Tanzania	1,000
Net Tax Liability	5,500

Note:

From the above figure of Shs. 5,500 must be deducted whatever personal relief(s) are available to Mr Njoroge, e.g. single relief, insurance relief, etc.

Example 48:

Basic facts as above but now assume that Mr Njoroge was charged tax amounting to Shs. 2,500 in Tanzania. Compute his net tax liability in Kenya.

In this case the maximum tax credit that can be given is:

	Shs.
Tax on total income (Kenya + Tanzania)	6,500
Less Tax on Kenya income alone	4,800
Maximum Double Taxation Relief	1,700

As Mr Njoroge paid Shs. 2,500 which is more than Shs. 1,700, he will be required to pay only that tax that is attributeable to his income from Kenya, i.e. Shs. 4,800. It is important to note that tax deducted in Tanzania (Shs. 2,500) should not be deducted from total tax (Shs. 6,500) if the resultant figure would be less than tax on Kenyan income alone.

Time Limit

Claims for Double Taxation Relief (or Tax Credit) must be made within six years from the end of the year to which the income relates.

QUESTIONS

1. Is withholding tax a special type of tax, levied on income received from sources other than employment?
2. What are the differences and similarities, if any, between PAYE system and withholding tax system?
3. What is meant by off-set of tax?
4. List the rates of withholding tax applicable to incomes received from various sources.
5. Find out from your nearest office of Income Tax the names of countries with which Kenya has a double taxation relief agreement.
6. Mr Sumburu earned £2,400 from sources in Kenya and £1,000 from sources in Uganda. Total tax deducted from his Ugandan earnings was Shs. 3,000. Calculate the amount of tax credit he can claim from Kenya, assuming that he is a Kenya resident.
7. Would your answer to Question 6 be any different if you were told that:
   (a) his income from Kenya sources was, in fact, only £900?
   (b) his income from Kenya and Uganda sources was as stated

in Question 6 but the amount of tax deducted from Uganda income was Shs. 7,400?

Chapter Twelve

ASSESSMENTS, OBJECTIONS AND APPEALS

ASSESSMENTS

Section 73 of the Income Tax Act states that the Commissioner of Income Tax will assess every person who is chargeable to tax as quickly as possible after the time allowed for delivery of the Return of Income.

When a person has delivered a Return of Income, the Commissioner may:

(a) either accept the Return as accurate and assess him on its basis,

(b) or if he has any reasonable cause to believe that the return is not true and correct, he may assess that person to the best of his judgement.

If a person fails to submit a return of income, the Commissioner has powers to determine his income to the best of his judgement and assess him accordingly.

If a person submits a Provisional Return of Income, the Commissioner will make a Provisional Assessment as soon as possible after the submission of such provisional return.

If the Commissioner has any reason to believe that a person is about to leave Kenya and that this person has not been assessed on any year of income, the Commissioner may determine his income to the best of his judgement and assess him accordingly.

ADDITIONAL ASSESSMENT

If the Commissioner feels that a person has been assessed at an income less than at which he ought to have been assessed, he may make an additional assessment.

TIME LIMIT

An assessment or additional assessment may be made any time before the expiry of seven years after the year of income to which the assessment relates, except:

(a) If fraud or wilful negligence has been committed by the person submitting a return of income. In this case an assessment can be made at any time.

(b) In the case of an assessment upon the executors or administrators of a deceased person, the period limit is three
years after the year of income during which the person
died.

BACK DUTY

This is the process whereby the Commissioner assesses a taxpayer
for any tax unpaid in any year of income in the past. The arrears
may arise either as a result of a taxpayer failing altogether to
notify the Commissioner of his liability, or of understating his
income in his return. In such cases the omission may be fraudulent or a result of negligence on the part of the taxpayer. If
so, as stated earlier, the Commissioner is empowered to go beyond
the usual time limit as he deems fit. Thus if the Commissioner
learns of a mistake, or wilful omission, in a return of income for
1971, in the year 1979, he will have every right and power to
issue an additional assessment and subject the taxpayer to a back
duty.

NOTICE OF ASSESSMENT

The Commissioner serves a notice of assessment on the person
assessed stating the amount of income, the amount of tax payable, and the rights of the taxpayer in relation to objection and
appeals.

WHEN ASSESSMENT IS NOT NECESSARY

The Commissioner of Income Tax is not required to assess a
person whose entire income is derived from an employment if
the total tax due from him has been deducted at source by way
of P.A.Y.E.

However, an employee has a right to apply to the Commissioner
to be assessed if he thinks that he has overpaid the tax, or for
any other reason. Such appeals must be made within seven years
after the year to which the income relates.

WHEN MAY COMMISSIONER REFRAIN FROM ASSESSING

Under Section 123 of the Income Tax Act, the Commissioner
can refrain from assessing or recovering tax from any person if:

(a) he is uncertain as to any question of law or fact,

(b) it will cause great hardship to the taxpayer, or

(c) it will be impossible to collect tax, or there will be undue
difficulty or expense in collection of tax.

When the Commissioner elects to refrain from assessing or recovering the tax in question the liability to such tax is deemed to be extinguished, or such tax is deemed to be abandoned or have been paid.

The Commissioner is required to report all such elections to the Minister before 30th June next after the date of his election. Thus if the Commissioner makes any such election during the period 1st July 1976 to 29th June 1977, he must notify the Commissioner before or on 30th June 1977. The Minister, upons receipt of such notification, may in writing direct the Commissioner to:

(a) take such action as the Minister may deem fit, or
(b) obtain the direction of the High Court upon the case.

OBJECTIONS TO ASSESSMENT

Section 84 of the Income Tax Act grants right to any taxpayer who is not satisfied with an assessment made upon him to lodge an objection in writing to the Commissioner. The objection must state the precise grounds on which it is based and must be received by the Commissioner within thirty days after the date of service of the notice of assessment. However, if the taxpayer is prevented from lodging an objection within this period by illness, absence from Kenya, or other reasonable cause, the Commissioner may, upon application by the person objecting and after he has deposited with the Commissioner the tax and interest due, or such part thereof as the Commissioner may require, admit the notice of objection.

On receipt of the notice of objection, the Commissioner may:

(a) amend the assessment as requested, or
(b) amend the assessment in the light of objection according to the best of his judgement, or
(c) refuse to amend the assessment.

If the Commissioner amends the assessment, whether as requested or otherwise, he sends an 'Amendment Notice'. If he refuses to amend the assessment he sends a 'Confirming Notice' to the taxpayer.

APPEALS AGAINST ASSESSMENT

If a taxpayer is dissatisfied with the Commissioner's decision on his objection, he may appeal to his area Local Committee or to the Tribunal within 30 days of receiving an amendment or confirming notice from the Commissioner. Appeals should be made to Tribunal if the assessment was, in the first place, raised on the taxpayer under Section 23 of the Income Tax Act (transactions designed to avoid tax liability) or under Section 24 of the same

Act (avoidance of tax liability by non-distribution of dividends). In all other cases the appeals should be made to the Local Committee. There is a Local Committee for every area covered by an Income Tax office. Resident persons should make their appeals to the area Local Committee for the area in which they reside whereas non-resident persons should appeal to the Local Committee for Nairobi area.

An appeal to the Local Committee or Tribunal may be made by giving a notice in writing to the Commissioner. If due to any acceptable reason (illness, absence from Kenya, etc.) a person fails to make the appeal within 30 days of receiving the Commissioner's decision on his objection, the Commissioner has the powers to demand the payment of the whole or part of the tax assessed and any interest due thereon before the appeal may be heard.

PROCEDURE OF LOCAL COMMITTEE APPEALS

Memorandum of Appeal

The appellant is, within thirty days of giving notice of his intention to appeal, required to submit a Memorandum of Appeal to the Clerk of the Local Committee. Eight copies of this document must be submitted. It must be signed by the appellant and state precisely the grounds of the appeal under distinct heads containing no arguments or narrative. The heads must be consecutively numbered. The Local Committee is not obliged to hear any evidence by the appellant or his agent which is not referred to in the Memorandum of Appeal. Documentary or other evidence should be referred to, including case-law where necessary.

The Memorandum of Appeal must be accompanied by:

(a)   A copy of the amending notice, or the confirming notice, or the notice of the decision of the Commissioner, as the case may be,

(b)   A copy of the notice of appeal, and

(c)   A statement signed by the appellant, setting out the facts on which the appeal is based.

On receipt of the Memorandum of Appeal, the Clerk of the Local Committee arranges the hearing after consulting the chairman of the Local Committee and gives notices thereof to:

(a)   each member of the Local Committee,

(b)   the Commissioner any every other respondent, and

(c)   the appellant.

Conduct of the Hearing

1.   The appellant is required to appear before the Local Com-

mittee either in person or by an agent on the day and at the time fixed for hearing of the appeal.

If the appellant is absent from Kenya, or is sick, or is prevented from attending at the hearing of the appeal due to some other reasonable cause on the day and at the time fixed for that purpose, the hearing may be postponed for a reasonable time.

2. The onus of proving that the assessment or decision appealed against is excessive or erroneous is on the appellant.

3. At the hearing the appellant or his agent is first allowed to state his case. After this the representative of the Income Tax Department is given an opportunity to state the views of his Department. The appellant is given a chance to reply to the remarks made by the representative of the Income Tax Department. Any witness may be called and cross-examined and re-examined by any party. The chairman and any member of the Local Committee may ask any questions of the appellant, respondent, or any witness at any time during the hearing. Copies of the documents can be produced as evidence, although the Committee has power to call for originals.

The Committee can adjourn the hearing of the appeal for the production of further evidence or for any other good cause.

4. The Committee (the Tribunal or the Court) has the right to confirm, reduce, increase, or annul the assessment concerned or make any such order as it deems fit.

5. The Local Committee is responsible for communicating its decision to the appellant and the Commissioner within seven days of the decision being made.

APPEAL AGAINST LOCAL COMMITTEE OR TRIBUNAL'S DECISION

If a taxpayer is dissatisfied with the decision delivered by the Local Committee or the Tribunal, he may, within fifteen days of being informed of the Committee or Tribunal's decision, appeal to the Court. The Chief Justice of Kenya has the powers to make rules to govern the proceedings of the Court in this respect.

An appeal to the court can, however, be made only on a question of law or of mixed law and fact.

The Commissioner of Income Tax has also the right to make an appeal to the Court if he is dissatisfied with the decision given by the Local Committee or the Tribunal.

LOCAL COMMITTEE AND THE TRIBUNAL

The Minister for Finance and Economic Planning may by giving notice in the Kenya Gazette establish a local committee for an area, or a tribunal. Local committees consists of a chairman and upto eight other members, whereas a tribunal may have a chairman and upto four other members, all appointed by the Minister. Each member serves for a period not exceeding two years, or as is specified in his appointment, unless before that time:

(a) he resigns by giving notice in writing, or

(b) the Minister is satisfied that the member is unfit because of some mental or physical infirmity to carry out his duties, or he has failed to attend three consecutive meetings, whereupon he may revoke his appointment.

The quorum for the Local Committee and Tribunal meetings is chairman plus two other members. Members are not personally liable for any act or default done by the Committee or the Tribunal in good faith.

The main function of the Local Committee is to hear any appeals arising within its area of jurisdiction except any appeals made on assessments that were in the first place made under Section 23 or 24 of the Income Tax Act. The main function of the Tribunal is to hear appeals from taxpayer in any part of the country against assessments made under Section 23 or 24 of the Income Tax Act.

RELIEF IN RESPECT OF ERRORS OR MISTAKES

If a taxpayer after having made a return, and after having been assessed on his return of income, discovers that he had made a mistake of fact in the return of income as a result of which he has been excessively assessed, he may, within seven years after the year of income to which the return relates, make an application to the Commissioner of Income Tax for a relief. On receiving such an application the Commissioner will inquire into the matter and after taking into account all relevant circumstances give such relief by way of repayment as he deems just, or refuse to give any relief. If the taxpayer is dissatisfied with the Commissioner's decision in this respect he may appeal to the Local Committee or the Tribunal in the same manner as he would have if he were dissatisfied with the Commissioner's decision on an objection raised by him on an original assessment.

No relief will, however, be given in respect of an error or mistake as to the basis on which the liability of an applicant should have been computed where the return of income was in fact made on the basis or in accordance with the practice generally prevailing at the time such return of income was made.

QUESTIONS

1. Under what circumstances may an additional assessment be issued by the Commissioner of Income Tax?
2. What recourse does a taxpayer who is dissatisfied with his assessment have?
3. What are the following terms used in connection with?
   (a) Back duty.
   (b) Amended Assessment.
   (c) Memorandum of Appeal.
4. When is it not necessary for the Commissioner of Income Tax to issue an assessment?
5. Describe the procedure of making an appeal to a Local Committee.
6. What is the main difference between local committees and a tribunal?
7. How is hearing conducted at local committee?
8. What recourse does a taxpayer who is not satisfied with the local committee's ruling have?

Chapter Thirteen

COLLECTION, RECOVERY AND PAYMENT OF TAX

TIME LIMITS

Sections 92 and 93 of the Income Tax Act specify the following time limits within which tax must be paid.

1. In case of final assessment the tax due from an individual person must be paid as follows:
   (a) If assessment is served before 31st May, 50% of the tax must be paid before 30th June and 50% before 30th September of that year.
   (b) If assessment is served after 31st May, the whole amount must be paid within 30 days of the notice of assessment.

2. In case of final assessment the tax due from a person other than an individual (e.g. a company, a trade association), must be paid as follows:
   (a) If assessment is served before 31st May, the whole amount of tax must be paid before 30th June of that year.
   (b) If assessment is served after 31st May, the whole amount of tax must be paid within 30 days of the notice of assessment.

3. If a provisional assessment is made on an individual, the amount of tax due must be paid in two equal instalments, the first within three months and the other within six months of the end of the accounting year of the taxpayer. Thus if the accounting year coincides with calender year, half of the tax is due by 31st March and the rest by 30th June of the year following the year of income. But if the accounting year runs from, say, 1st April to 31st March, the first instalment would be due on 30th June and the other on 30th September.

4. If a provisional assessment is made on a person other than an individual (e.g. a company) the whole of the tax is due within three months of the end of the accounting year of the taxpayer.

5. In the case of a company being wound-up the due date for payment of tax on the income for the preceding year and for the year of winding up is the day before the date of winding up order or resolution. Thus if a company passes a winding up resolution on 4th October 1978 and its accounting year ends on 31st August each year, the tax due for the year ended 31st August 1978 and for the year that commenced on 1st September 1978 will be payable on 3rd October 1978.

6. If a taxpayer has given a notice of objection but the objection does not dispute a part of the tax assessed, the amount not in dispute is payable in accordance with the provisions of the above paragraphs. Thus if a person has been served with an assessment notice asking for a tax payment of Shs. 3,500 before 30th June but he objects to the assessment declaring that as per his records the tax should be Shs. 2,800, then the latter amount is considered tax not in dispute. He must pay Shs. 2,800 before 30th June. The balance, which is in dispute, is payable as follows:

    (a) If the Commissioner agrees to amend the assessment in accordance with the objection, there will not be any amount due.

    (b) If the Commissioner amends the assessment and the revised assessment shows some tax due, that tax would be payable within 30 days of the notice of revised assessment.

    (c) If the assessment is determined on appeal (to Local Committee, Tribunal or Court), and it shows some tax due, it will be payable within 30 days of the notice of appeal's decision.

    The Commissioner has, however, powers to allow a taxpayer to pay less than the amount of tax not in dispute, or no tax, till he decides on his objection.

7. If a Local Committee, Tribunal or Court determines that a taxpayer has already paid any amount of tax that was not due from him, the amount so overpaid is refundable together with such interest as may be determined by the court.

8. The Commissioner has the power to extend the period within which any tax is to be paid and to specify another date of payment thereof.

Tax Due from a Deceased Person

If a person dies and any tax charged in assessment served to him prior to his death has not been paid, the amount due is payable out of his estate.

INTEREST ON UNPAID TAX

Section 94 of the Income Tax Act stipulates that if any amount of tax remains unpaid after due date, an interest of 5% shall immediately become due and payable thereon. If any amount of tax remains unpaid after the expiry of five months after the due date, interest of 5% will become due and payable. This interest will be calculated on the amount due plus interest already levied but is unpaid. Similar interest will become due and payable upon expiry of each succeeding period of five months on any amount of tax still remaining unpaid at each such expiration.

Example 49:

Tax of Shs. 10,000 is due from Mr Mwangi before 30th September 1977. If the tax is not paid on that date, 5% interest will be added to the tax and Mr Mwangi will be required to pay Shs. 10,500.
This amount is arrived at as follows:

	Shs.
Tax Due	10,000
5% interest on Shs. 10,000	500
	10,500

If Mr Mwangi pays up after 30th September 1977 but before 28th February 1978 (five months after 30th September 1977) he will be required to pay Shs. 10,500 but if he fails to pay it before this date, another addition of interest will be made and the amount due will be:

	Shs.
Tax Due	10,000
Interest for the first 5 months	500
Interest for the second 5 months @ 5% of Shs. 10,500	525
	11,025

If Mr Mwangi pays after 28th February but before 31st July 1978 he will have to pay Shs. 11,025 but if he pays after 31st July 1978 a further 5% interest on Shs. 11,025 will be added to the amount due.
The Commissioner of Income Tax has, however, the power to remit the whole or any part of any interest charged on unpaid

tax.

INTEREST ON UNDERESTIMATED TAX

If a person files a provisional return of income and is issued with a provisional assessment on it and later when he files a final return, the tax assessed on the final return turns out to be greater than the provisional assessment by 20% or more, he will be liable for an interest at the rate of 1% per month on the difference. Thus if a trader files a provisional return of income and is provisionally assessed at Shs. 30,000 but later on submission of his final return of income, the Commissioner assesses him at Shs. 40,000, tax @ 1% will be charged on Shs. 10,000.

However, if the Commissioner is satisfied that the difference was due to a reasonable cause, he may remit the whole or part of the interest that may be charged on the difference.

REPAYMENT OF OVERPAID TAX

Section 105 of the Income Tax Act states that if it is proved to the satisfaction of the Commissioner that a taxpayer has overpaid tax, such overpaid tax should be refunded to the taxpayer together with any interest payable under the Act. However, if there is tax outstanding for an earlier year of income, the overpayment is used to clear the outstanding tax and only the excess amount, if any, is refunded.

No repayment can be made if the overpayment relates to a period exceeding seven years before the year of income in which the claim for repayment is made. Thus if a person overpays any tax for 1971 and claims a repayment after the end of 1978 he will not be refunded any amount.

TAX RESERVE CERTIFICATES

These certificates are issued by the Treasury and carry interest. These may be purchased to set aside money for future tax liabilities and these can be used in payment of tax. The certificates are non-transferable. Interest earned on them is free of tax.

An employed person who has one or more sources of income other than emoluments from employment may have to pay a large amount of tax at the end of the year when his total income is assessed. He may buy tax reserve certificates during the year as he is able to do so, so that at the end of the year he is able to pay off his tax by surrendering the certificates instead of paying in cash. Buying these certificates is of course a means of saving money but they have an advantage over other methods of savings in that the interest earned by them is exempt from taxation.

COLLECTION OF TAX FROM PERSONS LEAVING KENYA

If a person who has been assessed to tax and has not yet paid it is about to leave Kenya, or has already left Kenya and his absence from Kenya is likely to be permanent, Section 58 of the Income Tax Act empowers the Commissioner to serve a notice on such a person requiring payment of the tax assessed or security for the payment. Thus if a person has been sent an assessment on 25th May and has been asked to pay the tax assessed by 30th September and he intends to leave Kenya before 30th September, the Commissioner will have the power to ask him to pay the tax due before leaving.

If a person fails to comply with the notice given by the Commissioner, the Commissioner may apply to a Magistrate for the arrest of that person. The magistrate will issue a warrant of arrest if he is satisfied that:

(a) an amount of tax is due and payable by such person,

(b) the person has failed to pay it, and

(c) there is reason to believe that the person is about to leave Kenya.

If the person is brought before the court and he fails to show just causes why he has failed to comply with the order, the magistrate may order him to pay the tax or give security and if he fails to do so, he may be sent to prison until either the tax due is paid or security given but not longer than six months. Such detention however does not release the person from his liability to pay tax.

TAX CLEARANCE CERTIFICATE

Section 99 of the Income Tax Act forbids transport operators to issue a ticket for travel abroad to any person who is not in a possession of a tax clearance certificate unless he is exempt from necessity to obtain a tax clearance certificate. Exempt persons are:

1. Persons entitled to diplomatic privileges.

2. Married women.

3. Individuals under 18 years of age on the date of departure.

4. Persons in East Africa on a visitor's pass.

5. A non-resident person in transit from a place outside the Partner States to a destination also outside Partner States.

6. Persons travelling on government duty.

7. Any other category of individuals as specified by the Minister by notice in the Kenya Gazette.

Normally assessments are raised at the end of an year of income but the Commissioner has power to assess a person at any time if he has any reason to believe that such a person is intending to leave East Africa. It is therefore necessary for any person wishing to leave East Africa (except those exempt) to obtain a tax clearance certificate from the Income Tax Department. The Commissioner will not issue such a certificate unless he is satisfied that all tax due from him has been paid or arrangements can be made to secure its payment. Generally for a non-exempt person to obtain a tax clearance certificate it is necessary for all tax due to be paid in full *and* to provide security for any tax not yet assessed. Thus if a person wishes to leave Kenya on 28th October 1977, he must pay in full any tax assessed on him for 1976 and if the Commissioner so asks, provide security for any tax that may be due for 1977 even though 1977 is not over by the time of his departure.

Security for tax may be provided in any one of the following forms:

   (a)   Lodgement of cash
   (b)   Purchase of tax reserve certificates
   (c)   Banker's guarantee
   (d)   Bond by an employer, or other person of acceptable standing
   (e)   Charge on real property.

Tax Clearance Certificate is granted by way of stamping it on the passport of the person wishing to travel and it remains valid for the period specified therein. Some businessmen and employees may, by nature of their business or duties, be required to travel very frequently. Subject to adequate security, such persons may be given long term clearance certificate by the Income Tax Department enabling them to make several departures from East Africa within the specified period.

The Commissioner may, by giving notice in writing, cancel any Tax Clearance Certificate, the cancellation being effective from the date of notice.

If security is given for payment of tax in the form of guarantee and the taxpayer defaults, the Commissioner may, by giving a notice in writing, require the guarantor to pay the tax within 90 days. The liability of the guarantor however ceases when the person who was given a tax clearance certificate on his guarantee returns to Kenya.

APPOINTMENT AND DUTIES OF AN AGENT

Section 96 of the Income Tax Act empowers the Commissioner

to appoint any person to be an agent for another person for collection of tax by giving a notice in writing to both the principal and agent. Persons who may usually be appointed are bankers or employers. An Agent so appointed must pay the tax specified in the notice out of the money held by him for the principal at any time during the twelve months following the date of appointment.

If any agent claims to be unable to comply with the appointment order because of lack of money held by him for the principal or any other reason, he should notify the Commissioner accordingly giving full reasons for his inability to comply. On receiving such notice, the Commissioner may:

(a)   either accept the notification and cancel the appointment, or

(b)   if he is not satisfied with the reasons given, reject the notification in which case the agent must carry out his duties.

It should be noted that an agent is required to pay tax to the Commissioner on behalf of the principal only if he is in possession of any monies that belong to the principal.

If an appointed agent fails to pay any amount of tax specified in his appointment notice to the Commissioner within 30 days of the date of such notice, or if he held no money for the principal at the time of receipt of appointment notice, within 30 days of the date on which any money belonging to his principal comes into his hand, the provisions of Income Tax Act relating to collection and recovery of tax apply to him as if the tax was due and payable by the agent.

Any person who claims to be unable to comply with the appointment notice will be guilty of an offence if he wilfully makes any false or misleading statement or wilfully conceals any material fact.

QUESTIONS

1.   What time limits, if any, exist for payment of tax assessed?
2.   How is interest due on unpaid tax calculated?
3.   What are Tax Reserve Certificates?
4.   What is a Tax Clearance Certificate? When and by whom is it necessary to be obtained?
5.   List the persons exempt from obtaining a tax clearance certificate.
6.   Explain the duties of an agent appointed by the Commissioner of Income Tax for tax collection purposes. Can a person so appointed refuse to accept the appointment?

Chapter Fourteen

OFFENCES AND PENALTIES

OFFENCES

Part XII of the Income Tax Act deals with offences and penalties. In general the following persons are deemed to have committed an offence under this Act:

1. A transport operator who issues a ticket to a non-exempt individual without such a person having obtained a tax clearance certificate.
2. Any person who tries to leave Kenya without a tax clearance certificate unless he is exempt for this purpose.
3. Any person who fails to submit a return of income, or who submits a return that is incomplete and inaccurate.
4. Any person who fails to submit relevant supporting documents.
5. Any person who fails to keep books of accounts or records or who destroys, damages or defaces such accounts and documents.
6. Any person who fails to attend at a time and place directed by the Commissioner, local committee, tribunal or court, without a lawful excuse.
7. Any person who fails to answer any question lawfully put to him or to supply any information lawfully required of him under the Income Tax Act.
8. Any person who discloses any confidential information on either income of a taxpayer or office documents of the Tax Department. (See paragraph on Official Secrecy later in this chapter).
9. Any person who accepts, or gives, bribe to help a taxpayer reduce his tax liability. (See paragraph on this offence later in this chapter).

TIME LIMIT FOR PROSECUTION

(a) Generally no prosecution for the above offences can be instituted at any time after two years of the commission of the offence.

(b)   Where books of accounts are not kept, or are destroyed, or damaged, prosecution can be instituted within two years of the date on which the Commissioner of Income Tax first learns of the commission of offence.

(c)   Any person who without a reasonable cause makes an incorrect return of income, or makes incorrect statement in a return of income can be prosecuted within six years of the date of the offence.

PENALTIES

(a)   Any person guilty of an offence under the Income Tax Act for which no penalty is specified is liable to a fine not exceeding Shs. 4,000 or to imprisonment for a term not exceeding six months, or to both such fine and imprisonment.

(b)   Any person who submits a fraudulent return to claim repayment of tax or to evade paying tax is liable to a fine not exceeding Shs. 10,000, (or double the amount of the tax evaded, whichever is the greater) or two years' imprisonment, or both.

(c)   Any person who offers bribes to a person to assist him in evading or reducing tax liability, and any person who accepts such a bribe is liable to a fine not exceeding Shs. 10,000 or three years' imprisonment, or both.

(d)   Any person who reveals any secret information will be liable to a fine not exceeding Shs. 10,000 or three years' imprisonment, or both.

(e)   If a person is punished for an offence, he still remains liable to pay the full amount of the tax and interest due thereon.

OFFENCES COMMITTED BY CORPORATE BODIES

If an offence is committed by a corporate body, every person who is a director, secretary, general manager, or any other similar officer of the body, at the time of commission of the offence is guilty of it unless he can prove that it was committed without his consent or knowledge and that he exercised such diligence as was necessary to prevent the offence from being committed.

POWER OF COMMISSIONER TO COMPOUND OFFENCES

If a person has committed an offence under the Income Tax Act and had admitted it in writing, the Commissioner has power, under Section 114 of the Act, to compound such an offence with approval from the Minister of Finance and Economic Planning. He may then order the offending person to pay a fine not exceeding the fine that would have been imposed on him if he were tried in a court.

When the Commissioner compounds any offence, the person who has committed that offence cannot be prosecuted for that offence.

OFFICIAL SECRECY

Section 125 of the Income Tax Act requires every person employed in carrying out the provisions of the Act to treat all documents and information relating to the income of any person as confidential. He should also treat as secret all confidential instructions in respect of the administration of the Income Tax Department which may come into his possession or to his knowledge in the course of his duties.

No person employed in carrying out the provisions of the Act can be required to produce any documents or give any information to the court unless it is necessary for the purpose of carrying into effect the provisions of the Income Tax Act.

The officers or employees of the Income Tax Department can reveal any document or information in the following cases:

(a) To another officer or employee in the course of his duties, or to another person authorised by the Minister.

(b) Solely for revenue or statistical purposes to any person in the service of the Government or of the Community in a revenue or statistical department.

(c) To the Controller and Auditor General, or to any authorised member of his department, where such document or information is needed by him for performance of his official duties.

(d) To any officer of a foreign government if any special arrangement is made for the allowance of (double taxation) relief from income tax in respect of the payment of tax in Kenya.

PENALTY FOR CONTRAVENING SECTION 125

Any person employed in carrying out the provisions of the Income Tax Act who:

(a) directly or indirectly asks for or takes any reward in connection with any of his duties, or

(b) enters into any agreement to do, abstain from doing, permit or conceal any act or thing whereby the tax revenue is or may be defrauded, or

(c) reveals to any person any document or information which comes into his possession or to his knowledge in the course of his official duties

is guilty of an offence and liable to a fine not exceeding Shs. 10,000 or three years' imprisonment, or both.

Any person who directly or indirectly offers or gives any employee of the Tax Department any payment or reward whatsoever, or proposes or enters into an agreement in order to induce him to do, abstain from doing, permit or conceal any act or thing whereby the tax revenue is or may be defrauded, or which is contrary to the provisions of the Income Tax Act is guilty of an offence punishable by a fine not exceeding Shs. 10,000 or three years' imprisonment, or both.

GENERAL

Upon an application by the Commissioner, a magistrate may give him the following powers provided he (the magistrate) is satisfied that there are reasonable grounds to suspect that an offence has been committed:

(a) To enter any premises between sunrise and sunset to search for money or documents.

(b) To open or remove from such premises any container, box or package in which it is suspected that money, documents or relevant articles are contained.

(c) To seize such money or documents for the purpose of any civil or criminal proceedings and to retain them for as long as they are required.

Signed receipt must be given to the suspected person for any document or articles seized. In the case of documents held by a banker, the power is limited to the making of copies or extracts therefrom.

Any person authorised by the Commissioner to enquire into the affairs of any person suspected to have committed an offence will at all times have full and free access to all lands, buildings and places and to all books and documents which he considers relevant to such inquiry and may make extracts from or copies of such books and documents.

QUESTIONS

1. Draw up a two-column chart. In the first column list the offences (under the Income Tax Act). In the second column list, against each offence, the penalty prescribed for that offence by the Act.

2. What is meant by compounding an offence?

3. Are there any time limits during which prosecution must take place?

4. How are offences committed by corporate bodies treated?
5. Briefly explain the provisions of the Section 125 of the Income Tax Act that deals with official secrecy.

Chapter Fifteen

CAPITAL GAINS TAX

WHAT IS CAPITAL GAINS TAX?

This tax is levied on gains arising on sale or transfer of certain assets, mainly property comprising of land and constructions thereon and marketable securities. It will be noted that a gain arising under such circumstances cannot reasonably be termed as a usual trading or business gain and hence is not included in the Profit and Loss Account of a business, or the return of income by an individual. Two points need particular attention here. Firstly, if an asset is sold at a profit, the profit may arise in the following two ways:

(a) The amount realised on disposal is more than the written down value of the asset but less than its cost. In this case, the surplus is called Balancing Charge. Balancing Charge has been explained in the Chapter on Capital Allowances.

(b) The amount realised on disposal is more than the cost of the asset. In this case, two gains arise. The excess of amount realised on sale over the cost of the asset is called 'Capital Gain', and the excess of cost over the written down value of the asset is termed Balancing Charge. For example, an industrial building that had cost £40,000 but had a written down value of £30,000 was sold for £48,000. In this case the excess of cost (£40,000) over written down value (£30,000) is Balancing Charge which is taxable as a normal business income. But the excess of amount realised on sale (£48,000) over cost (£40,000), i.e. £8,000 is a Capital Gain which is taxable at Capital Gains Tax rates.

Secondly, Capital Gains Tax, though different in nature from income and corporation tax, has been incorporated within the Income Tax Act in such a way that capital gains can be treated as a normal income provided tax attributeable to these gains does not exceed 35% of the gains in the case of individuals and 45% in the case of incorporated bodies. The following three examples will explain this point.

Example 50:

John Gathuru earns an annual salary of £900 from his employment and has no other source of income. In 1978 he made a capital gain of £2,500. Calculate his gross tax liability for 1978:

	Shs.
Basic Pay	900
Capital Gain	2,500
Taxable income	3,400
Tax on £1,200 @ 2/- per £	2,400
£1,200 @ 3/- per £	3,600
£1,000 @ 5/- per £	5,000
Tax on £3,400	11,000

In this example, tax attributeable to capital gains is at a rate less than 35% of gain, or Shs. 7 per £.

Example 51:

David Siele earned a salary of £6,800 in 1978 and also made a capital gain of £2,500 in the same year. Calculate his gross tax liability.

In this case, it will be better to calculate tax on salary and capital gains separately.

	Shs.
Tax on salary: On £1,200 @ 2/- per £	2,400
£1,200 @ 3/- per £	3,600
£1,200 @ 5/- per £	6,000
£1,200 @ 7/- per £	8,400
£1,200 @ 9/- per £	10,800
£ 800 @ 10/- per £	8,000
On £6,800	39,200

If Capital gain is added to salary, tax on capital gain would go into the bracket of the rate of Shs. 10/- per £ and above. But the Act provides that for an individual capital gains tax is restricted to 35%. Calculated separately, David Siele's capital gains tax liability would be:

Capital Gains Tax: On £2,500 @ 7/- in £ = Shs. 17,500.

Total Tax liability would thus be	Shs.
Income Tax	39,200
Capital Gains Tax	17,500
Total	56,700

Example 52:

George Luka earned a salary of £2,800 and made a capital gain of £4,000 in 1978. Calculate his tax liability.

In this case, we will notice that a part of the capital gain would be taxed at less than 35% rate because Mr Luka's salary does not reach this rate, but a part at 35% rate, even though the sum of salary and capital gain would exceed this rate if taken jointly.

			Shs.
Tax	: On £1,200 @ 2/- per £		2,400
	£1,200 @ 3/- per £		3,600
	£ 400 @ 5/- per £		2,000
Tax on Capital Gains	: £ 800 @ 5/- per £		4,000
	£3,200 @ 7/- per £		22,400
Tax on sum of salary and capital gain (£6,800)			34,400

The above three examples clearly demonstrate that Capital Gains Tax may be at a rate of less than 35%, or at the rate of 35%, or part at less than 35% and part at 35%, but never more than 35%, in the case of individual. In the case of incorporated bodies, e.g. companies, the difference between corporation tax and capital gains tax is less significant because both are calculated at 45%. It will therefore not be of any special value to keep a distinction between the two when calculating the tax liability. The situation would, however, be different in case there is a net business loss, or a capital loss, because a business loss cannot be off-set against capital gains, nor can capital losses be off-set against business profits.

DEFINITIONS

Capital Gain may be defined as 'the excess of adjusted transfer value over the adjusted cost of a property or marketable security or investment shares, arising on transfer of these items'. To fully understand this definition it is necessary to get a clear meaning of the terms involved, namely adjusted transfer value, adjusted cost, transfer of property, etc.

Property

Capital gains, for the purpose of calculating capital gains tax, are deemed to accrue only on the transfer of the following items:

(a) Property which includes land and any buildings, etc. attached to it and any other rights e.g. mining rights. It also includes any vegetation, forest, agricultural plants, etc. standing on land.

(b) Quoted shares. These shares are those issued by such companies or local authorities that are quoted and traded at the Nairobi Stock Exchange. These are also called investment shares.

(c) Unquoted shares. These include shares in companies not quoted at the Nairobi Stock Exchange.

(d) Other Marketable securities, e.g. debentures in a company not quoted at the Nairobi Stock Exchange.

No capital gain is deemed to accrue on the transfer of the following property items:

(a) Shares in the stock or funds of the government of Kenya, or the High Commission or the Authority established under the East African Community. (The authors wish to point out that at the time of this book going to press, no amendment had been made in the Act to take account of dissolution of the East African Community.)

(b) Shares of a local authority.

(c) A private residence if the individual owner has occupied it continuously for the three years immediately prior to the transfer. In ascertaining the period of occupancy any temporary absences may be ignored.

(d) Land transferred by an individual if:
  (i) the transfer value is not more than Shs. 30,000.
  (ii) the land is an agricultural property having an area of less than 100 acres and it is situated outside an urban area.

(e) Land which has been adjudicated under the Land Consolidation Act or the Land Adjudication Act when the title to such land has been registered under the Registered Land Act and transferred for the first time.

(f) Property which is transferred or sold for the purpose of administering the estate of a deceased person where such transfer or sale is completed within two years of the death of the deceased or within such extended time as the Commissioner of Income Tax may allow in writing.

Transfer of Property

A transfer of property is interpreted as follows:

(a) If a property is sold, exchanged, given, whether or not for a consideration. This implies that property transferred as a gift is also considered as a transfer for the purpose of

computing capital gains.
(b) If a property is lost or destroyed, whether or not compensation is received, unless the compensation received is used to install a new property in the same form and at the same place within one year.

There is no transfer of property for the purpose of computing capital gains in the following cases:
(a) Where the property is transferred temporarily to secure a debt or the transfer back again to the owner after the debt has been settled.
(b) When a company issues its own shares or debentures to its own shareholders.
(c) Where the property of a deceased person is vested in his legal representative by the operation of law.
(d) When the property of an incorporated body, e.g. a company, is vested in a liquidator for the purpose of winding up or bankruptcy.
(e) When the property is transferred on amalgamation of two or more companies, or on separation of amalgamated companies, provided such amalgamation or separation is in the interest of the country.

Transfer Value

Transfer value of a property means:
(a) The value of the consideration received for the transfer of property, or
(b) The amount received in return for the abandonment, surrender or forfeiture of the property, or
(c) The amount received for compensation for damage to or loss of property, whether from an insurance company or otherwise, or
(d) The amount received as consideration for the use of exploitation of the property, or
(e) In case where a person sells a property held by him as a security against loan given to another person, the amount by which the liability of the borrower is reduced, plus the amount paid to the borrower out of the proceeds of sale of property. For example Mr A owes Mr X a sum of Shs. 100,000 and has pledged an industrial building, Mr X sells the building for, say, Shs. 125,000 and after recovering his loan and expenses, etc. pays Shs. 20,000 to Mr A. For the purposes of calculating capital gain to Mr A, the transfer value of the industrial building sold would be the

sum of Shs. 100,000 (the amount by Mr A's liability has been reduced) plus Shs. 20,000 (amount received by him from proceeds of sale), i.e. Shs. 120,000. Now if the building had been bought for less than Shs. 120,000, the difference would be termed as a capital gain.

From the above transfer value may be deducted expenses incidental to disposal of property, e.g. advertisement, legal charges, to arrive at the adjusted transfer value.

Adjusted Cost

Adjusted cost includes the following:
  (a) The amount of consideration given for the acquisition or construction of the property.
  (b) Any expense incurred on the property to enhance or maintain its value.
  (c) Any expenditure incurred in preserving or defending the owner's title of the property.
  (d) Any incidental cost incurred in acquiring the property, e.g. legal fees, stamp duty, advertising, valuer's fees, etc.

No amount can be allowed as an adjusted cost or incidental cost if it has already been allowed as a deduction in computing profit chargeable to tax. Thus any amount spent on repairs cannot be treated as an adjusted cost if it has already been charged to the Profit and Loss Account as an expense.

If property is transferred or acquired together with other properties as one bulk, the Commissioner of Income Tax has the powers to determine what part of the adjusted costs or incidental expenses should be allocated to which part of the property and his decision is binding on both the buyer and the seller. However if any of them wishes to dispute the Commissioner's allocation he can appeal to a Local Committee.

If a property is transferred by way of a gift, or for consideration that cannot be valued, or as a result of a transaction between related persons, or in any other way other than a bargain at an arm's length, the amount of consideration for the transfer is taken as the market value of the property. The Commissioner has the right to determine the market value of such properties. Again, an aggrieved party can appeal to a Local Committee.

Example 53:

Francis Karanja bought an industrial building on 1st February 1975 for £50,000 and spent a total of £10,000 on making improvements on it. He also paid £2,500 by way of legal charges, stamp duty, valuation of property, etc. Three years later he sold the property for £70,000. Out of the proceeds he paid 1½% sales commission to the estate agent and £500 for other related expenses. Calculate the amount of capital gain.

			£
Cost of the Property			50,000
Improvements thereon			10,000
Incidental costs			2,500
Adjusted Cost			62,500
Transfer Value			70,000
Less Incidental Costs:	Sales Commission		
	@ 1½%	1,050	
	Other related		
	expenses	500	
			1,550
Adjusted Transfer Value			68,450
Less Adjusted Cost (as above)			62,500
Capital Gain			5,950

Maximum Tax on Capital Gain @ 35% of £5,950 = £2,082

SPECIAL REDUCTION

Tax on capital gains was introduced in the budget presented in June 1975. It became effective on 1st January 1975 for incorporated bodies and on 1st June 1975 for individual persons. A property sold before these dates for respective persons is free from any tax on capital gains. The Act also provides that a property bought before 1st January 1975 and sold before 1st January 1985 is entitled to a special reduction in computation of capital gains. This reduction is calculated as follows:

(a) Capital gain is computed in the normal manner (as shown in the Example 53).

(b) From the capital gain is deducted a percentage of it to arrive at chargeable capital gain. The percentage to be deducted is calculated by using the following formula prescribed in the Act:

$$\text{Reduction in \%} = \frac{1975 - A}{B - 1954} \times 100$$

In the above formula numbers 1975 and 1954 are constant. Letter 'A' stands for the number of the year in which the property is bought, but if the property was bought in or before 1955, letter 'A' stands for 1955.

Letter 'B' stands for the number of year in which the property is sold.

Example 54:

A property was bought in 1963 and sold in 1978. Calculate the percentage by which the capital gain would be reduced.

$$= \frac{1975 - A}{B - 1954} \times 100$$

$$= \frac{1975 - 1963}{1978 - 1954} \times 100$$

$$= \frac{12}{24} \times 100 = 50\%$$

Whatever capital gain results on the sale of the above property, it would be reduced by 50% to arrive at chargeable capital gain.

Example 55:

A house was bought in 1956 for Shs. 20,000 and sold in 1976 for Shs. 180,000. Calculate the maximum tax on capital gains assuming that the house was owned by an individual.

Step 1: Calculate the percentage by which the capital gain would be reduced, as follows:

$$\frac{1975 - 1956}{1976 - 1954} \times 100 = \frac{19}{22} \times 100 = 86\%$$

Step 2: Calculate the amount of capital gain as follows:

	Shs.
Transfer Value	180,000
Less Cost	20,000
Capital Gain	160,000

Step 3: From the capital gain calculated above, deduct 86% to arrive at chargeable capital gain.

	Shs.
Capital Gain	160,000
Less Reduction @ 86% of 160,000	137,600
Chargeable Capital Gain	22,400

Step 4: Now calculate the maximum tax on chargeable capital
gain @ 35% of Shs. 22,400 = Shs. 7,840.

Example 56:

A person bought a house for Shs. 100,000 in 1952 and spent
Shs. 25,000 on essential improvements. In 1979 he sold it for
Shs. 300,000. Assuming that his salary and other income is
already in a tax bracket of over Shs. 7/- per £, calculate the
tax on capital gain.

Note: In this case Letter 'A' will be taken as 1955.

$$\frac{1975 - 1955}{1979 - 1954} \times 100 = \frac{20}{25} \times 100 = 80\%$$

		Shs.
Transfer Value		300,000
Less Adjusted Cost	100,000	
	25,000	125,000
Capital Gain		175,000
Less Reduction @ 80% of Shs. 175,000		140,000
Chargeable Capital Gain		35,000

Maximum Tax on Chargeable Capital Gain @ 35% = Shs. 12,250.

Withholding Tax on Capital Gains on Property

The Income Tax Act places obligation on the purchaser of the
property to deduct 10% of the sale price of the property and
remit it to the income tax department. This however does not
constitute the tax on capital gain. The seller of the property
should then calculate the gain on transfer of the asset to the
satisfaction of the Commissioner of Income Tax, compute the
tax thereon and remit the difference or claim the refund. The
following two examples will demonstrate this procedure.

Example 57:

Jack Njohi sold an industrial building for £24,000 in 1978.
He had bought it for £21,000 in 1975. Calculate the amount
of withholding tax, tax attributeable to capital gain assuming
that his earnings from other sources are £4,000 in 1978, and
the amount of refund he should claim from the Commissioner
of Income Tax.

Sale Price, £24,000.
Withholding Tax @ 10% of Sale Price, £2,400.

Capital Gain, £3,000 (£24,000 - £21,000)
Tax on Capital Gain @ 35% = £1,050.

Refund to be claimed	£
Withholding Tax	2,400
Less Tax on Capital Gain	1,050
Over-deduction	1,350

Note: As Mr Njohi's earnings from other sources, £4,000, are already in a tax bracket of Shs. 7 per £, the whole of capital gain will be taxed at 35%.

Example 58:

Robert Wahiu bought a second house in 1975 for £20,000. In 1978 he sold it for £31,000. His earnings from other sources amounted to £5,100 in 1978. Compute the amount of withholding tax, tax on capital gain, and the amount by which the latter exceeds the former.

	£
Sale Price	31,000
Withholding Tax @ 10% of sale price	3,100
Capital Gain (£31,000 - 20,000)	11,000
Tax on Capital Gain @ 35%	3,850

Tax on Capital gain (£3,850) exceeds withholding tax (£3,100) by £750 which amount must be paid by Robert Wahiu to the Tax Department when he is sent his assessment for 1978.

CAPITAL GAINS ON SALE OF SHARES AND SECURITIES

The basic principles governing computation of capital gains on sale of shares and securities are similar to those for properties, except in the following respects:

(a) The adjusted cost of shares is taken as the cost plus stamp duty and brokerage.

(b) The transfer value of shares is arrived at by deducting broker's commission and related expenses from the sale price.

(c) Shares are usually handled by brokers who are members of the Nairobi Stock Exchange. These brokers act both as buying and selling agents. Thus a person wishing to invest money in shares is likely to buy them through a broker and if he decides to sell them he would sell them through the same broker. The brokers, therefore, are in a position to calculate capital gain on every deal made by them on behalf of their clients. The Income Act therefore places an obligation on the broker acting on behalf of the seller to deduct tax at 35% of capital gain and pay the balance to the seller. He must remit the tax so withheld to the Commissioner of Income Tax. Compare this with the position in regard to properties where the withholding tax is 10% of the sale price.

Example 59:

Albert Karuru bought some shares for £500 on 1st July 1975, paying £4 as stamp duty and £6 as commission. He later sold them for £600, paying £20 as commission to the broker.

	£	£
Transfer Value	600	
Less Broker's commission	20	
Adjusted Transfer Value		580
Cost of Shares	500	
Stamp Duty	4	
Broker's commission	6	
Adjusted Cost		510
Capital Gain		70

Capital Gains Tax to be deducted by broker @ 35% on £70 = £24.
Amount to be paid by the broker to Karuru = £556 (£600 - 20 - 24).

Treatment of shares bought before 13th June 1975

The provisions for tax on capital gains that were introduced in Finance Bill were first made known on 13th June 1975. The Act specifies that any shares that were bought before that date would be deemed to have been bought at the market value prevailing at the Nairobi Stock Exchange at the close of business on 12th June 1975. The brokers are required to calculate capital gain (or loss) on any shares sold by them on behalf of their clients after 13th June 1975 on the assumption that they were bought at the cost prevailing on 12th June 1975. However, if a person selling shares can prove to the satisfaction of the Commissioner of Income Tax that he had, in fact, paid more for the shares than their market value on 12th June 1975, he can claim a refund from the Commissioner, not the broker.

Example 60:

Jack Nganatha bought 1,000 shares at Shs. 24 per share on

10th June 1975. The market value of these shares dropped to Shs. 22 per share on 12th June 1975. He sold them at Shs. 30 per share on 3rd March 1978. Ignore incidental costs.

	£
Transfer Value (1,000 x 30/-)	1,500
Less Market Value on 12.6.1975 (1,000 x 22/-)	1,100
Capital Gain	400

Tax to be deducted by broker @ 35% on £400 = £140.

Later, Mr Nganatha can apply to the Commissioner of Income Tax for a refund, submitting proof that he had bought the shares at 24/- each.

The refund will be calculated as follows:

	£
Transfer Value	1,500
Less Cost (1,000 x 24/-)	1,200
Capital Gain	300

Tax on Capital Gain @ 35% on £350 =	£105	
Tax deducted by broker	140	
Refund to be claimed	£ 35	

CAPITAL LOSSES

Capital losses arising out of transfer of property or shares can be off-set against capital gains arising in the same year but not against business profits or personal income. If no capital gain has been made in the year in which a capital loss arises, the capital loss can be carried forward and off-set against capital gains in future years.

CAPITAL GAINS MADE BY COMPANIES

All the examples solved in this chapter related to capital gains made by an individual. In the case of companies the rate of tax on capital gains is 45% of the gains which, for Kenya registered companies, is the same rate as for corporation tax. Calculation of tax on capital gains must however be shown separately from Profit and Loss Account. If a company holds controlling shares in another company, then in the event of sale of such shares, a goodwill may arise. Such goodwill is also treated as a capital gain.

QUESTIONS

1. Define and explain the following terms:
   (a) Capital Gain.
   (b) Transfer Value.
   (c) Adjusted Cost.
2. Define and explain the following terms:
   (a) Property.
   (b) Marketable securities.
   (c) Investment shares.
3. Mr Odindo earned a salary of £1,200 and made a capital gain of £1,000 in 1978. Calculate his tax liability for 1978.
4. Mr Odede earned a salary of £1,800, made a business profit of £1,000 and a capital gain of £2,000 in 1978. In the same year Mrs Odede earned a salary of £900. Calculate Mr Odede's tax liability for 1978.
5. Mr Odera earned a salary of £1,400 and Mrs Odera earned £1,200 in 1978. In the same year they made a capital gain of £3,000. Calculate Mr Odera's tax liability for 1978.
6. List the capital gains that are exempt from tax.
7. Mr Omar bought an industrial building for £24,000 in 1975. In the same year he spent £6,000 on its improvements. Legal costs, stamp duty, etc. incidental to purchase of property amounted to £500. He sold the property in 1978 for £45,000, less 1½% sales commission of the estate agent. Calculate the amount of capital gain and the maximum tax payable thereon.
8. Basic facts as for the above question, but now assume that the property was in fact bought in 1969. Calculate the maximum tax on capital gain.
9. Basic facts as for the Question 7, but now assume that the property was bought in 1953. Calculate the maximum tax on capital gain.
10. Abubakar bought a second house in 1968 for £10,000 and spent £2,000 on carrying out improvements. He had also paid £1,000 by way of incidental costs (e.g. valuers' fees, lawyers' fees, stamp duty, etc.) He sold the house for £20,000 in 1979. His income from other sources in 1979 was only £300. Calculate:
    (a) Capital Gain.
    (b) Withholding Tax deducted by the person who bought the house from Abubakar.
    (c) Any repayment or additional tax resulting in 1979. (use 1978 rates for tax computation.)

11. Said Bin Bakar bought an industrial building for £20,000 in 1963. In 1978 he sold it for £80,000. His income from other sources in 1978 amounted to £4,100. Calculate:
    (a) Capital Gain.
    (b) Withholding tax deducted by the buyer in 1978.
    (c) Any repayment or additional tax resulting in 1978.
12. Musa Ali bought 500 shares of £1 nominal value at £1.20 each on 1st July 1975. He paid broker's commission at 5% and stamp duty at 1%. He sold them at £2 each in 1978. Calculate:
    (a) Capital Gain.
    (b) Withholding tax deducted by broker.
13. Akbar Ali bought 800 shares at £2 each on 1st August 1975. He paid 10% brokerage and 5% stamp duty. He sold 600 of them in 1978 at £4 each. Calculate:
    (a) Capital Gain.
    (b) Withholding tax deducted by broker.
14. Basic facts as for Question 13. Now assume that Akbar Ali in fact sold the shares at £1.60 each, and calculate:
    (a) Capital Gain or Loss.
    (b) Withholding tax to be deducted by broker.
15. Basic facts as for Question 13. Now assume that the shares had been issued by a local authority. Calculate capital gain or loss, and the amount of withholding tax that should be deducted by broker.
16. Atiq Qureshi bought 1,000 shares in a quoted company as follows:

Purchase price	£2 per share
Date of purchase	10 May 1975
Market Value on 12.6.1975	£1.80 per share
Incidental Costs	£10 on 1,000 shares.

    He sold all of them in 1978 at £2.40 per share. Calculate:
    (a) Capital Gain.
    (b) Withholding Tax deducted by broker.
    (c) Amount of refund that he can claim from the Commissioner of Income Tax.
17. Basic facts as for Question 16. Now assume that Mr Atiq Qureshi had in fact paid only £1.50 per share for the shares. Calculate:
    (a) Capital Gain.
    (b) Withholding Tax deducted by broker.

APPENDIX

Past K.A.S.N.E.B. Examination Papers

Note:

The following rates should be used for all questions in this appendix.

Chargeable Income £	Rates Shs. in £
1—1200	2/=
1201—1800	3/=
1801—2400	4/=
2401—3000	5/=
3001—3600	6/=
3601—4200	7/=
4201—4800	8/=
4801—5400	9/=
5401—6000	10/=
6001—6600	11/=
6601—7200	12/=
7201—9000	13/=
On all Total Income over £9000	14/=

Wear and Tear Allowances:

Class I	37½%
Class II	25%
Class III	12½%

CPA PART II
TAXATION II (Old Syllabus)
TAXATION (New Syllabus)
October 1977

1. Explain any three of the following terms for the purposes of the Income Tax Act, Cap. 470.

"Whole time Service director."
"Permanent Establishment."
"Resident" when applied in relation to an individual.
"Management or professional fee."
"Trade Association."

2. Mr I.M.A. Cooker, helped by his wife, runs a tea house cum snack bar on University Way, patronised mostly by students. He submitted his Return of Income for 1976 showing losses of £1,234. In support of this figure, the following Receipts and and Expenditure account and information were submitted:—

Expenses	£	Receipts	£
Purchase of groceries etc.	6,215	Sale of food etc.	15,645
Wages to staff	3,912	Juke box collection	1,903
N.S.S.F. and P.A.Y.E.	360	Sale of old cooker	
Gas and electricity	613	and furniture	211
New Cooker	216	Charity Sweepstake	
Salary to wife	900	winnings	650
Rent and Rates	2,200	Loss	1,234
Uniforms, cleaning material,			
flowers etc.	319		
Utensils and Crockery	216		
Repairs and renewals	816		
Insurances	430		
Legal Expenses	316		
Household expenses including			
school fees	2,215		
Car-running Expenses	915		
	19,643		19,643

The family lives in the flat above the business premises; the rent is apportionable 2/5th flat and 3/5th the tea house.
Insurances include premiums amounting to £140 in respect of Cooker's life insurance policy.
It is estimated by Cooker that personal use of the car is about 40% of the total mileage.
Cooker has not yet paid the rent (£200) for December and

shop grocery bills amounting to £316.

Analysis of Repairs and renewals:

	£
Painting and Decoration	216
New furniture	418
Repairs to toilets	182
	816

There was, at the beginning of the year, stock of groceries, tinned food, soft drinks amounting to £115 and at the end, £96.

You are required to:

(a) Calculate the adjusted profit/loss for the year for income tax purposes, ignoring any second schedule deductions that may be due.

(b) Explain all the assumptions made in arriving at the adjusted profit, and

(c) Make any enquiries and comments that you consider necessary.

3. George Kinuthia, a qualified civil engineer has submitted his Final Return of Income for the year ended 31 December 1976 with the following information:—

		£
Adjusted profit from practice		6,321
Gross Dividends on E.A. Brewery shares		150

	£	£	
Gross Rents received		1,500	
Less Rates and Insurance	123		
Painting and Repairs	300		
Cost of extension to garage	800		
		1,223	277

His wife is employed as a cateress with a well known hotel of international standard at a salary of £200 p.m. (total P.A.Y.E. deducted Shs. 6,000/-) — 2,400

She is entitled to free dinners for two every month (customers pay £3 for a four course dinner) and 3 free overalls annually, each costing £6.

Mr Kinuthia has three children as follows:—

Michael born on 14 April 1967, Jane on 3 October 1972 and Peter on 10 May 1977.

Michael goes to St. George's School, State House Road, Jane attends the Greengate Nursery School. Mr Kinuthia paid insurance premiums as below:—

Name of Company	*Person Insured*	*Amount*	*Type of Insurance*
		Shs.	
Cannon Insurance Co.	Self	3,000	Life
J.H. Minet & Co.	"	1,200	Personal Accident
Jubilee Insurance Co.	Son	1,500	Education

In July 1976 his wife attended an auction sale and purchased a set of antique chairs and table for £300 which she resold for £900 thereby making a gain of £600.

Calculate Mr Kinuthia's tax liability for the year and state the dates on which he is required to make payments.

4. Write *fully* on any *one* of the following:—

   (a)   Gains on Transfer of property (8th Schedule).
   (b)   Chargeability of non-residents.
   (c)   Ascertainment of Income of Resident Insurance Companies. (Section 19).
   (d)   Avoidance of Tax (Sections 23 and 24).

5. Aromatic Tea Limited grows tea near Kericho and processes the green tea leaves in its own factory. During the year 1976 the company, under an expansion programme, incurred the following capital expenditure for which claims have been lodged for deductions under the Second Schedule:—

	£
Agricultural land for planting tea bushes	8,000
Irrigation plant	3,200
Nursery shed for transplanting	1,532
Labour lines for tea pickers	3,218

Factory and Offices

	£
Cost of land adjacent to existing factory buildings	5,000
Additions to existing factory buildings (including a small office block costing £1,730)	18,500

Machines installed in above additions to factory buildings

		£
(1)	Dehydrating Plant (new)	4,216
(2)	Conveyer belt (secondhand) but fixed to (1) above	815
(3)	Grading machine (new)	1,840
(4)	Moveable Avery Scale (new)	600
(5)	Mobile Fork Lift (secondhand)	2,100

Vehicles

	£
2 Lorries to transport tea leaves to the factory for processing	8,900
Peugeot 404 Saloon car for the Supervisor's use	4,800

Furniture and fittings

	£
in the new office block and factory buildings	812

Calculate the second schedule deductions which are due to the company on the above expenditure.

CPA PART II
TAXATION II (Old Syllabus)
TAXATION (New Syllabus)
March 1977

1. Explain, with reference to the Income Tax Act 1973 (and Amendments), what is meant by any *three* of the following terms:—
   (a) Tax Clearance Certificates.
   (b) Local Committees and Tribunals.
   (c) Double Taxation Relief.
   (d) Collusive Agreement of hiring.
   (e) "Housing Deduction."

2. Lake Fish Packers Ltd., a company (based in Kisumu) processing and packing fish fillets, started its operations in January 1975. It had incurred the following capital expenditure:

	£
Cost of Land	8,000
Cost of Buildings (including cost of Administration and office block £8,000)	54,000
Second hand processing plant (installed in the above buildings)	19,000
Packing machine (installed in the above buildings)	8,250
Moveable weighing scale	750
Loose Tools and implements	500
2 Delivery vans and a saloon car (£3,600, £3,000, £4,200 respectively)	10,800
Furniture and Fittings in office and administration block	1,250

Calculate the deductions due to the company under the Second Schedule for the year 1975.

3. David Kang'ethe holds 1,600 £1 Ordinary Shares in Fine Fabric Manufacturers Ltd. (Authorised and Issued Share Capital £30,000) and drew a salary of £450 per month in 1975 as the Company's Chief Accountant and was paid £1,200 as director's fees. (Total PAYE deducted Shs. 50,000/=). He was provided

with free housing and a company car (benefit valued at £200) throughout the year. He is also a member of the company's pension scheme to which the company contributed £240 in the year. A gross dividend of 10% was declared and paid by the company on 31st December 1975.

He has five children. The eldest, on completion of his secondary education, started serving articleship in September 1975 and was paid £40 per month. The second and third, both under 18 years of age, attend school throughout the year. The youngest was born in March 1975. He paid the following Life Insurance premiums:

Name of Company	Capital Sum	On whose Life	Premium paid in Kenya Currency
	Shs.		Shs.
Pan African	40,000	Eldest son	600
Norwich Union	80,000	Self	2,200
Prudential Assurance	75,000	Wife	1,900

Calculate Mr Kang'ethe's tax for 1975.

4. Leatherette Ltd., manufacturers of shoes, handbags and other leather goods, submitted its Final Return for 1976 (accounting date 30th June) with, among other documents, the Trading and Profit and Loss Accounts as below:—

	£		£
To stock at 1.7.1975	15,290	By sales (Less Returns)	272,567
" Purchases	126,672	" stock at 30.6.76	19,265
" Salaries, Wages and Training Expenses	65,983	" Profit on Exchange	1,236
" Electricity and Water expenses	6,567	" Profit on Sale of Shares	735
" Insurances	3,456	" Dividends (from a wholly owned subsidiary company)	1,000
" Rents, Rates and Taxes	12,340	" Interest Received	212
" Vehicle Running Expenses	6,728	" Net Loss	4,025
" Travelling Expenses	4,295		
" Contributions to N.S.S.F.	1,987		

	£		£
To Pensions Bonus and Gratuity	16,732		
" Bank charges and Interest	1,398		
" Repairs and Renewals	9,820		
" Subscription and Donations	416		
" Legal Expenses	995		
" Postage and Telephones	1,267		
" Bad debts	3,529		
" Depreciation	9,167		
" General Expenses	12,398		
	£299,040		£299,040

Appropriation a/c

	£		£
To Net loss b/d	4,025	By unappropriated profit b/f	13,675
" Directors fees	7,200	" accumulated loss c/f	5,350
" Proposed Dividends	7,800		
	£19,025		£19,025

The following further information and schedules were attached to the profit and loss accounts:—

Bad debts include an increase in general provision of £1,325.

Legal Expenses were in respect of:

	£
Renewal of lease of factory premises for 6 years	125
Issuing notices to defaulting trade debtors	370
Drawing up letter of Hypothecation for overdraft facilities	250
Purchase of private house for a director	250
	995

Rents, Rates and Taxes include £4,210 paid to the Collector of Income Tax in settlement of the Company's tax for the year 1975.

Training Expenses An amount of £3,000 was for a director's son studying overseas, with the intention of eventually being employed by the company.

Interest received was on a deposit account in a London Bank.

Pensions amounting to £1,235 were paid to retired staff.

During the year a Ford pick-up costing £3,850 was purchased to replace an old motor van which was traded in for £1,100. The net price was included in *Vehicle running expenses.*

Analysis of Subscriptions and Donations

	£
Annual Subscription to Association of Leather Goods Manufacturers	120
Annual Subscription to Kenya National Chamber of Commerce	96
Payments to Dr. Barnado's Home and Salvation Army	200
	£416

You are required to:—

(a) Compute the adjusted profits as far as possible for income tax purposes, ignoring any wear and tear deductions that may be due.

(b) Indicate any further enquiries that you wish to make.

5. Write all you know about any *one* of the following:—

(a) Gains on Transfer of Property (Eighth Schedule)
(b) Members Clubs and Trade Associations (Section 21)
(c) Exemption from Tax (Section 13, 14 and 1st Schedule)
(d) Time Limit for making assessments (Section 79).

CPA PART I (Old Syllabus)
TAXATION I
April 1977

1. "Green Pastures Farm" is the name under which N. Njoroge
and K. Kamau carry on dairy farming in equal partnership. The
accounts for the year to 31st March 1976 show a *loss* of £735
after including/charging the following:—

	£
Wages (including £2,400 to each partner)	15,500
Depreciation	6,230
Legal Expenses for purchase of Kamau's residential house	212
Bad debts written off	335
School fees for both partners' children	290
Bank charges and interest on overdraft	516
Chemical and fertiliser	1,113
Purchase of delivery van	4,000
Interest received on Tax Reserve Certificates	32
Dividends (gross)	150
Sale proceeds of old Peugeot pick-up	1,315
Miscellaneous income (sale of vegetables, etc.)	639

The partners consume milk, vegetables etc. the total value of
which was considered to be £480.

From the above information calculate the share of profit of
N. Njoroge and K. Kamau. The written down value of assets as
at 31st March 1975 were as follows:—

Class I	Class II	Class III
£	£	£
6,395	13,466	658

Details of Farm Works Total cost of Fences, Dips etc. in 1974
£8,500.

2. Write short notes on any *three* of the following:—
   (a) "Management or Professional Fees"
   (b) Insurance Relief
   (c) Provisional Return

(d) Scientific Research
(e) Assessment on a deceased person.

3. Winston Wanjohi, an employee of Look Smart Limited, manufacturers of gents, ladies and children's clothing, forwarded the
following particulars in his Return of Income for 1976:—

$$£$$

Salary   5,000)
Commission   360) P.A.Y.E. deducted Shs. 35,000/=

Value of shirts, dresses and baby clothes provided by employer £240.
Free housing was provided for the whole of the year.
Insurance premium paid by employer £210.
His wife was employed as a personal secretary and earned
£1,800 (PAYE deducted Shs. 8,000/=). She holds some E.A.P.
& L. shares and received gross dividend of £120 from which
withholding tax was deducted at the appropriate rate. She
also received (as a Christmas present from her boss) a leather
handbag and matching shoes valued at £60.
They support and maintain 3 children of their own, all under
16 years of age and Winston's brother aged 17 years.

Calculate the tax payable by Mr Winston Wanjohi for the year
1976.

4. State, *giving reasons for your decision,* the assessability or otherwise, of the following:—

(a) Value of medical benefits (£200) enjoyed by an employee
under a scheme operated by his employer.
(b) Samuel Smith, a resident of the U.K. owns a residential
house (in Lavington, Nairobi) which is let at £150 per
month.
(c) Michael Macharia was credited with the following amounts
of interest:
£30 on a Savings bank account in Tanzania.
£50 on a Deposit account with a London Bank.
(d) "Eastleigh Sports Club" had the following income:—

	£
Fees and subscriptions from members	1,500
Interest on Savings a/c	25
Donations	30

Total expenditure in running the club was £1,510.

(e) Gross Dividend received by A. Company (Kenya) Ltd. from B. Company Ltd. in which it holds 2,500 shares. The latter company (having an authorised and issued share capital of £10,000 in £1 shares) operates in Thika.

(f) Tips received by a bar-attendant.

5. Calculate the Industrial Building Deduction which a manufacturing company (accounting date 31st December 1975) is entitled to on capital expenditure incurred in 1975 on the following:—

		£
	Cost of Land	3,600
(	Cost of Factory Building	19,200
(	" " Office and Adminis-	
Brought into use	tration Block	3,250
w.e.f. 1.8.1975	(Cost of Store and Packing	
	Shed	5,000
	(Cost of Sports pavillion and	
	Club house for employees	2,500

CPA PART I
TAXATION I
October 1976

1. I. Pullem, a dentist, has been in practice for several years in premises on Reata Road. He is married with 2 children, born on 19th July 1971 and 6th February 1975. He submitted the following Income and Expenditure account for the year 1975 in support of his Return of Income for that year:—

	Shs.		Shs.
Salaries and wages (includes			
Shs. 1,000 p.m. drawn by self)	29,200	Fees from services	80,328
N.S.S.F Contributions	1,300	Income from Overseas	
Donations and subs to sports		Investments	5,100
clubs	120		
Car running expenses	3,678		
School fees for elder child	3,600		
Household expenses	12,015		
Rent—Reata Road	9,600		
Bank charges	320		
Light and Water—Reata Road	1,160		
Telephone and postages	1,210		
General expenses (all allowable)	3,516		
Excess of income over			
expenditure	19,709		
	85,428		85,428

His wife works as a Secretary in a soft drinks manufacturing company and received £1,500 as salary plus free soft drinks for the family for the whole year, valued at £96. On Christmas Day her boss gave her a picnic hamper worth £60 as a Christmas present. P.A.Y.E. deducted from her salary amounted to Shs. 3,000.

You are required to calculate the tax payable by Mr I. Pullem for the year 1975. 50% of car-running expenses is attributed to private use. The written down value of his car was £1,216 as at 31st December 1974.

2. John Joshua Kamau, who was resident in Kenya for the whole of 1975, submitted a Return of Income for the same year showing the following particulars:—

Gross Salary from Good Home Construction Company Ltd.

£225 p.m. from 1st January 1975 to 31st March 1975 and £250 p.m. from 1st April 1975 to 31st December 1975. In addition he was provided with living quarters for the whole of 1975. P.A.Y.E. was deducted from his salary amounting to Shs 11,000/=.

His wife, a teacher in a secondary school earned £1,200 during the year, from which P.A.Y.E. deducted was Shs. 2,500/=. They have 3 children all under 18 years of age and attending full-time school.

Mr Kamau holds some Brewery shares and received £180 gross dividend from which withholding tax was deducted at 15%. He also has a Life Insurance Policy on which he paid premiums totalling £200 in 1975.

Calculate net tax payable by him for the year 1975.

3. Write explanatory notes on the following:—

   (a) Housing Deduction
   (b) Tax Clearance Certificate
   (c) Provisional and Final Returns
   (d) Exemption from Tax
   (e) Deductions under Parts I to Parts V of the Second Schedule to the Income Tax Act 1973.

4. Better Road Builders Limited had the following assets with written down values as below:—

	Class I £	Class II £	Class III £
Written down value 31st December 1974	23,352	15,344	4,596

During the year of Income 1975 the following were purchased and sold:—

A catterpillar (heavy earth-moving vehicle) was purchased for £15,000 and a light lorry for carrying stone, sand etc. was sold for £3,500. It was replaced by a Bedford lorry costing £6,500. The new office block was furnished at a cost of £3,000 and some old furniture was sold for £1,500.

Calculate the wear and tear deductions the company may claim under Second Schedule to the Income Tax Act 1973.

5. Explain what rights under the provisions of the Income Tax Act, 1973, a tax payer has in the following circumstances:—

  (a) An estimated assessment made by the Commissioner which the taxpayer considers not to be in accordance with his income for that year.

  (b) The Commissioner refuses to amend an estimated assessment and issues a notice confirming the assessment raised on a taxpayer.

What precise actions must the taxpayer take to ensure that he is assessed on a proper basis?

CPA PART II
TAXATION II
April 1976

1. Johnathan David Githae buys and sells properties in order to make a living. The following were his transactions during the year of income 1975. You are required to calculate his income for tax purposes:—

	£
Five houses bought for	65,000
Repairing costs etc.	3,000
Decoration charges	1,200
Legal Fees	
Stamp duty, drawing up Title Deeds, etc.	3,500
Entertainment	200
Interest on loan	3,200

The houses were all sold in 1975 for £17,500 each. Mr Githae has a car, written down value at 1.1.75 £3,200, which he uses in supervising the buying and selling, and arranging to see potential customers, etc. He reckons that 50% of the car running is for business purposes. His total car-running expenses in 1975 were as follows:—

	£
Petrol and oil	120
Repairs	200
Tyres and spares	132
Licence and Insurance	300
	752

2. (a) Outline fully the provisions of the section of the Income Tax Act dealing with claim for relief under error or mistake.

Answer any *one* of the following:—

(b) What redress does a tax payer have at his disposal if he is not satisfied with the assessment made on him?

(c) What is meant by withholding tax? State in your own words how it operates and how set-off is granted.

3. The 1975 Return of Income of Kenya Ropes and Twines Ltd., had attached among other documents, the following Trading

and Profit and Loss Account for the period ended 30th April 1975.

	£		£
To Opening Stock	13,260	By Sales	295,670
" Purchases	110,982	" Closing Stock	23,238
" Wages	62,359	" Profit on Sale of	
" Insurance	5,282	Plant and Machinery	22
" Contributions to Retirement		" Sub-letting rent	720
Benefits	1,813		
" Provident Fund	1,307		
" Legal Expenses	1,295		
" Advertisement	2,635		
" Salaries & Commissions	33,563		
" Bank Charges	623		
" Bad debts	1,567		
" Repairs and replacements	9,372		
" General Expenses	2,389		
" Subscriptions (£293) and Donations (£230)	523		
" Vehicle Running Expenses	23,456		
" Lease Rent & Rates (including staff housing)	15,586		
" Christmas gifts to staff	637		
" Travelling Expenses	15,320		
" Depreciation:			
Plant & Machinery 2,348			
Vehicles 1,623	3,971		
" Delivery Van Scrapped	538		
" Net Profit	13,172		
	319,650		319,650

APPROPRIATION ACCOUNT

	£		£
To Directors fees	8,000	By net profit b/f	13,172
" Proposed Dividend (gross)	10,000	" Unappropriated	
" Profit c/f	3,495	Profit b/f	8,323
	21,495		21,495

In reply to queries you obtain the following information:—

(a) "Purchases" include the cost of a machine £5,000 installed during the year.

(b)   *Analysis of legal expenses*

	£
Stamp duty on increased authorised Share Capital	900
Renewal of lease (less than 99 years)	100
Recovery of Trade debts	295
	1,295

(c)   "Bad debts" include an increase in general provision of £630. The rest of the amount represent actual bad debts written off.

(d)   Repairs and replacements include £4,500 the cost of a delivery van to replace the one written off during the year.

(e)   General Expenses were for:

	£
Cleaning materials	356
Pension paid to a retired member of staff	1,200
Papers and periodicals	123
Cash loan to a customer written-off	710
	2,389

(f)   Travelling expenses include £6,000 air fare for director's wife and a child when they accompanied him on his business trip to an overseas country.

(g)   Plant costing £4,000 in 1971, book value £2,258, was sold during the year.

Written down value of assets as at 30.4.74 are as follows:—

Class II	Class III
£	£
18,565	25,328

You are required to draw up the Wear and Tear Schedule and calculate the 1975 adjusted income for income tax purposes.

4. Joseph Kamau Kinama is the technical director of Super-Clean Soap Factory Ltd., holding 500 ordinary shares out of issued share capital of 16,000 shares of £1 each. During the year 1975 he was paid a salary of £450 per month with free housing for part of the year (August 1975 to December 1975) and free use of car for the year valued at £120. During January to July he lived in his own house which was subject to a mortgage loan of £11,000 at 9% interest. He let his house from August 1975 at £95 rent p.m. The expenses of the house were as follows:—

	£
Mortgage Interest	990 (for the whole year)
Repairs and Decorating prior to letting	500
Agents fees	150
Gardener — full year	180
Rates — ” ”	600

During the period he was not occupying his house he was paid House Allowance amounting to £80 p.m.

His wife worked as the personal secretary to the manager of Kenya Fruit and Vegetable Exporters Ltd., and earned £2,400 per annum. Besides, she was given a supply of fruit, eggs and vegetables for the whole year, valued at £260. She had a Christmas bonus of £150 paid in cash from the Company and received a hamper valued at £100 from the manager as a personal Christmas Gift.

Mr Kinama is a member of the Company's Medical Scheme and free treatment valued at £200 was afforded to him during the year. He has three children, all of them under 18 years of age and maintains his orphaned brother aged 16. He had the following insurance policies:—

Name of Company	Capital sum Shs.	On whose life	Premium paid in Kenya Currency Shs.
Jubilee Insurance Co.	80,000	Self	800
Cannon Assurance	75,000	Wife	600
Old Mutual	60,000	Eldest son	400

Dividend at 10% gross on issued Share Capital was paid on 31st December 1975 by the Super Clean Soap Factory Ltd.

Calculate Mr Kinama's tax for the year 1975 taking into consideration the following P.A.Y.E. deducted from his and his wife's salaries:

> Self: Shs. 16,000
> Wife: Shs. 10,000

and

Withholding tax on Dividend.

5. A sellotape manufacturing company at Thika incurred the following capital expenditure on 28th February 1975 (accounting date 30th June 1975).

	£
Factory Buildings (including value of land £6,500)	90,000
Installations of the following machinery in the factory building	
Heat and Pressure Detector Plant	658
Cutting and gumming machine	13,765
Packing unit	6,500
	20,923

Production started on 1st March and you are required to calculate the deductions the company may claim in arriving at the adjusted profit for 1975, for tax purposes and the residue of Industrial Building as at 30th June 1975.

CPA PART I
TAXATION I
April 1976

1. Answer the following questions, and explain your reasoning for the answers given:—

   (i)   Sam Smith has been living in Kenya for eight months during 1975. He is engaged on market research, and receives a monthly salary in £ sterling from his employer, a firm which has no residential status in Kenya. Is Sam liable to Kenya income tax on his salary, and if so, on how much of his salary?

   (ii) Tony Thomas is an overseas cabaret star due to visit Nairobi for a three week engagement. Will he be liable to Kenya income tax, and if so, how is this calculated?

   (iii) United Limited is a non-resident company which receives a management fee under a technical service agreement with Kenya Company. Is this liable to Kenya income tax, and if so how is this calculated?

   (iv) Ventures is the registered name of a Kenya partnership which has recently established a branch overseas. Will profits of the overseas branch be liable to Kenya income tax?

   If a double taxation agreement existed between Kenya and the country in which the branch operated what would be the significance of this?

   (v)   X is a members club. The club derives £2,000 income from members. In addition, it receives the following income from external sources:

   £50 rent of rooms
   £20 interest on a deposit account
   £30 advertising
   £20 hire of equipment.

   Expenses amount to £1,800. On what income is the club taxable?

2. Under Section 35 of the Income Tax Act 1973 withholding tax is deductible from certain income. For the following examples state whether in your opinion withholding tax is deductible and at what rate, assuming that payment was made in 1975.

   (a)   Management fees paid to a resident company.
   (b)   Interest Shs. 175 paid to a resident.

(c) Pension to an individual resident in Lusaka.

(d) Rent paid to a resident.

(e) Royalty paid to a manufacturer in Sweden.

Would your answer be any different if in all of the above questions payment was made to residents of Tanzania?

3. Section 15 of the Income Tax Act 1973 sets out deductions allowed in arriving at profits.

Paragraph (a) of Section 15 mentions bad debts incurred.

Under what circumstances may these be deducted?

State whether or not the following would qualify for deduction, giving your reasons:—

(i)   A trading company's loan to an employee which the employee, following termination of his employment, refuses to repay.

(ii) A trading company's loan to a retailer to enable him to purchase equipment for use in retailing the products of the lender and which the retailer, on disposing of his business, refuses to repay.

4. Using the Tables provided calculate the 1975 tax payable by a resident individual whose income consisted of:—

	£
Salary as Manager	4,000
Free use of company car, valued at £200	
Other benefits amounted to £300	
Wife's salary	1,500
Business income per accounts	1,225
Dividends paid net of tax	170
Government pension	400

5. (i)   An employee invests his savings in a taxi operation which proves profitable. He has never been required to complete tax returns in the past. Explain his obligations to do so following the change in his circumstances.

   (ii) Outline the procedure you would adopt in presenting an appeal to the local committee against an amended assessment confirmed by the Commissioner of Income Tax.

   What documents must be presented to the Local Committee?

   Outline the powers the Commissioner has on receipt of an objection.

6. (i)   An individual sells some property for £5,000 gross. How much withholding tax is deductible from such proceeds?

   (ii)   A company sells some property for £30,000. How much withholding tax is deductible from such proceeds?

   (iii)   A Kenya resident whose annual income exceeds £10,000 wants to plan his tax affairs for 1976. He has the opportunity of supplementing his recurrent income by selling some paintings. Assuming the profit on sale of paintings will be liable to tax either as a capital gain or as trading income, what advice would you give him?

7. A long established private company commenced manufacturing in Thika in November 1974. Its accounts for the year to 31st October 1975 show a profit of £130,845 after charging:—

	£
Depreciation	18,400
Donations	250
Pension contributions to Insurance Co.	2,560
Under provision for income tax 1974	225
Bad debts	926
P.A.Y.E. Penalty	25
Legal fees in respect of claims against the building contractor	750
Mortgage interest	1,860
Provision for leave pay	2,900
Lease hire instalments on director's car	800

The Profit included £180 interest on tax reserve certificates.

Capital expenditure incurred during the year was:—

	£
Factory building	61,000
Draughtsman's and factory manager's Office	5,625
Administrative offices	8,950
Machinery installed in factory	33,500
Self propelled crane	15,600
Fencing around factory building	3,140
Furniture	3,250
Car for General Manager	3,850

The written down values at 1st November 1974 were:—

Class I	Nil
Class II	7,800
Class III	11,250

Provisions for leave pay were:—

at 31st October 1974	3,100
at 31st October 1975	4,500

A director's motor car which cost £3,000 was sold for £2,600. No profit or loss on sale was recorded in the company's accounts.

From the above information

(a) prepare a tax computation and calculate the amount of tax payable, and

(b) calculate the minimum distribution to shareholders.